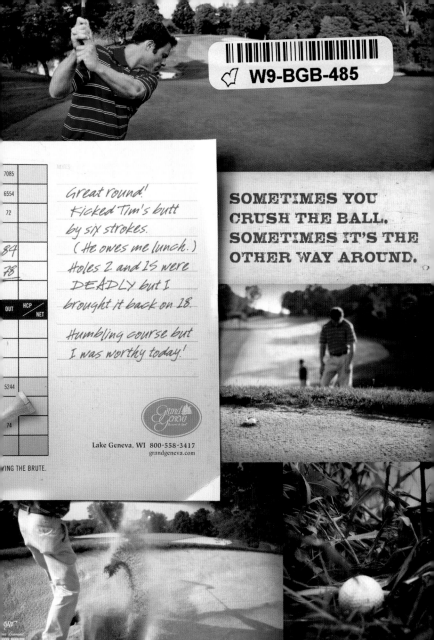

W9-BGB-485

NOTES:

7085	
6554	
72	

Great round!
Kicked Tim's butt
by six strokes.
(He owes me lunch.)
Holes 2 and 15 were
DEADLY but I
brought it back on 18.

Humbling course but
I was worthy today!

	HCP	
OUT		NET

5244	
74	

Grand Geneva
Resort & Spa

Lake Geneva, WI 800-558-3417
grandgeneva.com

WING THE BRUTE.

**SOMETIMES YOU
CRUSH THE BALL.
SOMETIMES IT'S THE
OTHER WAY AROUND.**

Golf Wisconsin

The Official Guide to the State's Top 25
Public Courses . . . Plus 50 More Fun Places to Play

GOLF
Wisconsin

The Official Guide to the
State's Top 25 Public Courses
. . . Plus 50 More Fun Places to Play

JEFF MAYERS AND JERRY POLING

J O N E S
B O O K S
Madison, Wisconsin

Jones Books
309 N. Hillside Terrace
Madison, Wisconsin 53705-3328
www.jonesbooks.com

First edition, first printing

The beautiful photographs for this book came from a variety of sources. Golf course photographers Paul Hundley (www.paulhundley.com) and Gary Knowles (OPENAIR@aol.com) were very generous. Hundley's photographs appear on pages 1, 3, 5, 7, 9, 11, 25, 27, 29, 41, 43, 61, 63, 65, 69, 71 and 85. Knowles' photographs appear on the Table of Contents page, pages 45 and 47 (Madeline Island) and 102 (Apostle Highlands). The aerial photo of Alpine Resort Golf Course on page 101 was provided by Door County Visitor Bureau (doorcounty.com). Other photographs were submitted by individual golf course owners and operators, chambers of commerce and visitors bureaus as well as the Department of Tourism (thanks to Jerry Huffman, who helped make the book possible) and its agency, Boelter + Lincoln (in particular Andy Larsen, who coordinated the final round of submissions). All were used with permission from the suppliers of the photographs.

Library of Congress Cataloging-in-Publication Data

Mayers, Jeff, 1959-
  Golf Wisconsin : the official guide to the state's top 25 public courses—plus 50 more fun places to play / Jeff Mayers and Jerry Poling.
      p. cm.
  Summary: "Describes with text and color photos Wisconsin's top 25 public golf courses, including the hole to beat at each course."
—Provided by publisher.
  ISBN 978-0-9790475-0-3
  1. Golf courses—Wisconsin—Guidebooks. 2. Wisconsin—Guidebooks.
I. Poling, Jerry, 1958- II. Title.
  GV982.W6M385 2007
  796.35209775—dc22

                              2007002842

Printed in China

TABLE OF CONTENTS

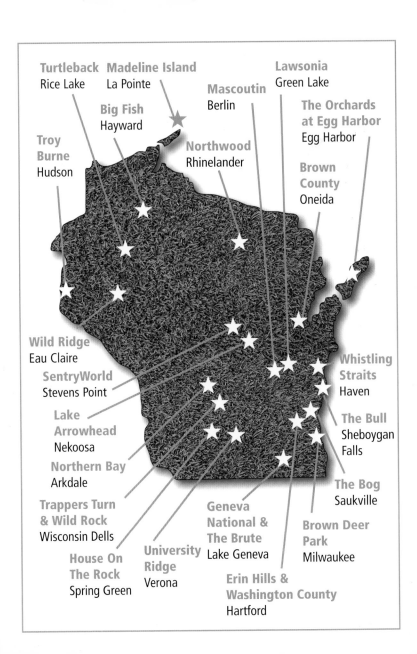

Introduction

Determining what's best when it comes to golf courses is a very subjective thing.

But after writing about and playing golf courses around the state for many years, we've come to agree on what we like about our favorite courses.

Forget the part about scoring well. After years of chasing pars, we're more often than not content for the bogey save and the occasional round in the low 80s. Of course, we'll always have a soft spot in our golfing hearts for a course where we somehow have put it all together.

We like courses that take us to pretty places, that provide a respite from a hectic world, that have some interesting history, that are designed by an architect who knows how to use the land not just bulldoze it, that give us a variety of challenges, that accept walkers, that pay attention to the details of greenskeeping, and that know how to serve customers.

In this book, we've tried to use some of those factors in detailing our list of the state's 25 best courses spread out around Wisconsin. We wanted to focus on the state as a whole and not just the 25 best courses to give you, the traveling golfer, a sampling of great golf from Lake Superior to Milwaukee.

In that, we're returning to the approach in the 1994 book, *Great Golf in Wisconsin*, by John Hughes and Jeff Mayers. Hughes now runs *Wisconsin Golfer* magazine, but Jerry Poling stepped in as co-author on *Wisconsin Golf Getaways*, a combination golf course and state attraction guidebook published in 2001.

Six years later, it's time to take another look at the state's best courses. There are plenty of new additions, but there are a few of the old favorites, too.

Some of you may wonder why your choice for a Wisconsin "best" isn't included. In some cases, it had to do with geography—with our quest to have courses in the major tourist areas of the state. There were indeed some close calls, but those things had to be done to get to the magic 25. To help remedy any omissions, we've gathered 50 more fun places to play in our final chapter.

So join us on this most excellent golf adventure, and may your drives always find the fairway.

Jeff Mayers and Jerry Poling

Big Fish Golf Club

HAYWARD

The city of Hayward may be small (population 1,900), but the people in this northwestern vacation mecca like to think big. The city and region boast of the National Freshwater Fishing Hall of Fame, the World Lumberjack Championships and the American Birkebeiner, North America's biggest cross country ski race, as well as other major events.

Add another big name to the list: Big Fish Golf Club. Opened in 2004, the course's name came out of the region's reputation for producing big fish, including the world's biggest musky. The name also could reflect the person the developers reeled in to design the course: world-renown architect Pete Dye, who designed, among many great courses, Wisconsin's Whistling Straits.

While Dye left some of his Straits-style craggy bunkers at Big Fish, it is only vaguely reminiscent of his Lake Michigan shoreline gem. With a Sawyer County piece of land that was half open and flat and

BIG FISH GOLF CLUB

4,938 to 7,079 yards
par 72
rating 73.4
slope 136

ARCHITECTS
Pete Dye, Tim Liddy

CALL
(715) 934-4770

WEB SITE:
www.bigfishgolf.com

ADDRESS
14122W True North Lane,
Hayward, WI 54843

DIRECTIONS
From U.S. Highway 27, take County B four miles east of Hayward. The course is at the junction of B and K, next to the LCO Casino.

half wooded and hilly, Dye and co-designer Tim Liddy essentially created two courses. The front nine at Big Fish is inland links and the back nine classic northwoods golf, similar to the Robert Trent Jones Jr. design at University Ridge near Madison.

Big Fish has all the trappings of a first-class Dye-Liddy course, numerous risk-reward holes, creative routing, well-positioned bunkers, target landing areas and collection areas around the large greens. "This course has the whole package," said Matt Vandelac, the head pro and one of the owners.

The front nine, with nary a tree and flatter than Whistling Straits, isn't imposing, but at the whim of the north wind and with strategically placed bunkers, it can pack plenty of punch. Holes to watch for include the par 4 fourth hole, which stretches to 517 yards; the par 5, 560-yard seventh, guarded most of the left side by a pond; and the short ninth, just 129 yards but to a narrow green that falls away to deep bunkers.

Dye and Liddy backed off a little on the back-nine bunkering, if only because they also had trees and hills on their palette. After a par 5, downhill 13th that offers a birdie opportunity, the last five holes put a premium on accuracy and shot-making. With wide landing areas, back nine holes are framed by, but not necessarily pinched by, thick stands of hardwoods.

Big Fish seems to get tougher the farther it recedes into

the woods. The 15th, a par 4 that runs 470 yards uphill, doesn't have a sand trap but doesn't need one. The 190-yard 16th tumbles over a sandy hollow in a secluded corner of the property. The par-5 17th has trouble lurking down the left side and around the well-bunkered, perched green. The 18th, 440 yards, emerges from the woods with a greenside pot bunker, a Dye trademark, and a view of the great northwoods.

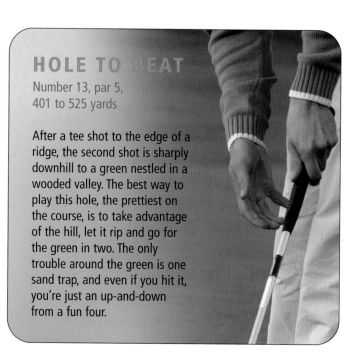

HOLE TO BEAT
Number 13, par 5,
401 to 525 yards

After a tee shot to the edge of a ridge, the second shot is sharply downhill to a green nestled in a wooded valley. The best way to play this hole, the prettiest on the course, is to take advantage of the hill, let it rip and go for the green in two. The only trouble around the green is one sand trap, and even if you hit it, you're just an up-and-down from a fun four.

The Bog
SAUKVILLE

After playing the first hole, a 530-yard par 5 with 20 bunkers, or after finding yourself in some of 15 old-styled Scottish bunkers on the course, you might think this venue should be called The Trap.

But after a round on this secluded layout winding around some 100 acres of wetlands, playing the 470-yard, par 4 15th (no traps but a tough hole usually into the wind), and seeing the largest peat land in southern Wisconsin on its western border, you'll know that The Bog was given the right name. That 1,700-acre peat land is called the Cedarburg Bog, and it's the central, natural feature that helps makes this a special place for golf.

Course founder Terry Wakefield finalized the vision back around 1990, and after bringing in Arnold Palmer and some others, he got the course he wanted by mid-1995—fast work considering the quality final product.

THE BOG

5,110 to 7,221 yards
par 72
rating 75.3
slope 143

ARCHITECT
Arnold Palmer with Ed Seay

CALL
(800) 484-3264

WEB SITE:
www.golfthebog.com

ADDRESS
3121 County Hwy I, P.O. Box 80079, Saukville, WI 53080

DIRECTIONS
Take Interstate 43 North to Highway 33 (exit 96), drive three miles west on 33, turn south onto County Road I and then one-quarter mile to entrance.

Wakefield, Palmer and friends must have done something right. *Golf Digest* annually ranks it as one of the best courses in the state.

The varied design melds with the natural feel of the course with its wildflower-filled meadows, groves of leafy trees and, of course, the wetlands. But don't be lulled by the bucolic setting.

This is a course that rarely yields low numbers. Palmer, back when he was still competing on the Senior Tour, shot a 74 from the back tees after the course opened (see more below in the Hole to Beat). But it can be done. Dave Spengler, a Wisconsin pro, scored a 65 during a U.S. Open Qualifier in May 2000.

For the rest of us, we'll be happy for a sprinkling of pars and a final score in the 90s—especially after the backbreaking finish. Start with that 15th hole, the longest par 4 on the course. Then to the 439-yard 16th, which doglegs 90 degrees left around water and brush wetlands. On to Number 17, at 593 yards, the longest and most demanding par 5 on the course; it's got water, sand, wetlands and an uphill approach. The 430-yard par 4 18th looks pretty from the tee, but is nothing but trouble if you don't hit it straight; Mole Lake is to the right, fairway sand is to the left and out of bounds is left of the green.

After this finish, bow to "The King" and to The Bog—a great golf combo.

HOLE TO BEAT
Number 12, par 4, 318 yards

The shortest par 4 on the course is the trickiest. Palmer took a triple-bogey 7 here on his way to a 74 in 1995 during the course's grand opening. Forget about going for the green, unless you can hit a high, 318-yard cut shot. The problem is a creek that cuts in front of the green. Even after a perfect layup over the right bunkers to a wide landing area, it's a knee-knocking 60-yard pitch over the stream.

Brown County
Golf Club
ONEIDA

When young architect Lawrence Packard finished Brown County Golf Club near Green Bay in August of 1958, some golfers said it was too tough. At more than 6,700 yards and with numerous hazards, it was more than recreational golfers were used to in the days of wood drivers and blade irons. It was so challenging that the next year it was picked to hold the State Open.

With modern golf equipment shortening courses, Brown County isn't considered a monster anymore, but it remains one of the state's best tests of golf. Packard's design, which subtly uses rolling terrain, stands of hardwood trees and two meandering creeks to test all aspects of a player's game, has withstood the test of time.

"I definitely consider it one of the top courses we've ever done," said Packard, originally a Chicago-based architect who went on to design many courses in Wisconsin, as well as the

BROWN COUNTY GOLF CLUB

5,801 to 6,749 yards
par 72
rating 72.1
slope 133

ARCHITECT
Lawrence Packard

CALL
(920) 497-7819

WEB SITE:
www.co.brown.wi.us/golf_course

ADDRESS
897 Riverdale Drive, Oneida, WI 54155

DIRECTIONS
From Green Bay on U.S. Highway 29/32 travel northwest until you reach County J; turn left (south) and proceed about four miles and then turn left over the railroad tracks.

acclaimed Innisbrook resort course near Tampa-St. Petersburg, Fla.

The front nine, which sets up better for golfers with a draw, has two tough par 4s. The 423-yard fourth doglegs left around and into a thick stand of trees and Duck Creek. The ninth, 444 yards, requires a long drive to the corner of the dogleg and a long, uphill second shot over Trout Creek to a green with plenty of slope.

The back nine, favoring golfers with a fade, starts with an Amen Corner of sorts—three tight par 4s that traverse the far, tree-lined corner of the property. The 11th is 444 yards. With a lovely view from the tee, it doglegs right downhill past trees. The 12th, 399 yards, runs next to Duck Creek and more trees. The finishing hole doesn't sound intimidating at 397 yards, but it can be a tough par. The hole plays uphill, turning right past mature oak trees at the corner. A shot too far left falls into Trout Creek valley.

A half-century after it opened, Brown County continues to challenge golfers, drawing not only the tax-paying county residents who own the course but golfers from across the state. The course, once listed among *Golf Digest* magazine's top 75 U.S. public places to play, held the State Boys Junior in 1999, the State Match Play in 2002 and the State Amateur in 2005. It was the first municipal course to hold the State Am in the more-than-100-year history of the event.

One county resident, Bob Barclay, had lobbied for the

course just before the game of golf experienced rapid growth in the 1960s, and has seen the investment pay off. "We knew we had an excellent site. (Packard) really convinced us it had everything. The course has proved it's true," Barclay said.

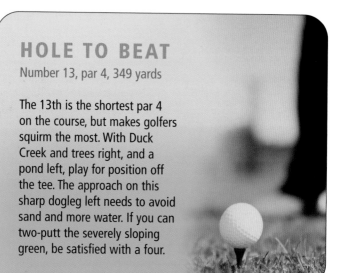

HOLE TO BEAT
Number 13, par 4, 349 yards

The 13th is the shortest par 4 on the course, but makes golfers squirm the most. With Duck Creek and trees right, and a pond left, play for position off the tee. The approach on this sharp dogleg left needs to avoid sand and more water. If you can two-putt the severely sloping green, be satisfied with a four.

Brown Deer Park

MILWAUKEE

Locals still stumble a bit and call it the GMO, for Greater Milwaukee Open.

What they should be saying is the U.S. Bank Championship, which has yet to acquire an easy abbreviation, but survived a PGA Tour reorganization to secure a July 19–22, 2007 slot.

And what they're talking about is the annual PGA Tour event that has been staged in Milwaukee since 1968.

It started at Northshore Country Club (with Dave Stockton winning the inaugural event) and stayed for two more years before moving to Tripoli Country Club for only two years then over to Tuckaway Country Club from 1973–93 (Stockton again winning the inaugural) before settling in at the venerable and comfortable municipal course, Brown Deer Park, beginning in 1994.

BROWN DEER PARK

5,861 to 6,759 yards
par 71
rating 72.9
slope 133

ARCHITECT
George Hansen

CALL
(414) 352-8080

WEB SITE
www.countyparks.com
(follow the "golf" link on the left)

ADDRESS
7625 N. Range Line Road, Milwaukee, WI 53209

DIRECTIONS
Exit I-43 at Good Hope Road north of downtown Milwaukee and travel west to Range Line Road; turn north to the course.

It's a good fit for a city that has usually been known more for bowling than golf. Winners of the championship befit the blue-collar image of the city still known as Brew Town and

home to Major
League Baseball's
Milwaukee Brewers
at Miller Park. Well,
you get the picture.
Many past winners
have been
journeymen pros
who never came close
to winning a major.
But Greg Norman is
a past winner (1989)
as well as Corey
Pavin (who won in

2006, a decade after his first Milwaukee win as part of sweet
comeback story) and others who have won one of the four
major golf championships. Past Milwaukee winners also
include great African-American golfers, Lee Elder and Calvin
Peete, 1978 and 1979, respectively.

Jack Nicklaus, Gary Player, Arnold Palmer, Tom Watson,
Lee Trevino and Sam Snead all played the tourney. But the
biggest GMO—er, U.S. Bank Championship—moment may
have been the rookie debut of one Tiger Woods in 1996. He
made an ace in the final round, a harbinger of things to come.

And so, as the advertising goes, you can play the course
Tiger and the pros have played.

What you'll find is a well-tended classic course tweaked
gently over the ages but still harboring thick stands of tall trees,
placid ponds and gentle slopes that typify the county park that
contains the course. The credit goes to George Hansen, the
longtime county parks superintendent who designed five of the
county courses in the early part of the 20th century. The best

of the lot is Brown Deer, which opened in July 1929 and hosted the U.S.G.A. Public Links Championship in 1951, 1966 and 1977 before falling into disrepair. But beginning in 1987, a $2.25 million facelift, including a redesign by Roger Packard and Andy North (the two-time U.S. Open winner from Madison), restored it to its former glory and improved upon Hansen's work. The uphill number 18 has become a 557-yard risk-reward hole that tempts the pros to try for eagle.

You can try, too, just like the pros.

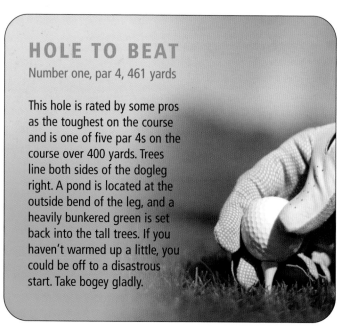

HOLE TO BEAT
Number one, par 4, 461 yards

This hole is rated by some pros as the toughest on the course and is one of five par 4s on the course over 400 yards. Trees line both sides of the dogleg right. A pond is located at the outside bend of the leg, and a heavily bunkered green is set back into the tall trees. If you haven't warmed up a little, you could be off to a disastrous start. Take bogey gladly.

The Brute
at Grand Geneva
LAKE GENEVA

The old Playboy Club and the old Briar Patch Course are gone, but the Brute remains a Wisconsin golf classic.

Built in the heyday of the Playboy Club days off a design by Robert Bruce Harris for about $1.8 million—really big dollars in 1968—the Brute still lives up to its name.

On a breezy day from the back tees (built to play at the then-unheard length of 7,200 yards), the Brute will take everything you've got. But enjoy the park-like surroundings, the grand Geneva-area views and some interesting local lore along the way as you play past the old "bunny dormitories" along the second fairway and a large abstract sculpture said to represent a frustrated golfer near the tough 190-yard par 3 16th hole.

Bob Hope performed here. So did Henny Youngman and Richard Pryor. Cher tried the putting green while wearing spiked heels. Tony Randall and Sammy Davis Jr. were on hand for the grand opening. "I gave lessons to Christie Hefner

THE BRUTE AT GRAND GENEVA

5,244 to 7,085 yards
par 72
rating 73.8
slope 136

ARCHITECT
Robert Bruce Harris

CALL
(888) 392-8000

WEB SITE
www.grandgeneva.com

ADDRESS
7036 Grand Geneva Way,
Lake Geneva, WI 53147

DIRECTIONS
Near the intersection of
U.S. highways 12 and 50
just east of Lake Geneva.

(Hugh's daughter) when she was just a little girl," recalled Ken Judd, the resort's longtime former pro.

Despite all the glitter around it, the Brute survived because it was in some ways ahead of its time. Its long and spacious layout is characterized by elevated tees and greens, massive putting surfaces, some 70 sand traps (some as big as a normal green) and plenty of water hazards.

Water comes into play sneakily on the tricky third hole, a 374-yard par 4. The fairway drops abruptly downhill, where two ponds pinch it to a narrow isthmus 250 yards from the tee. Use an iron off the tee and try to land it before the ponds. Then use a short iron onto the sloping green.

Staying out of the water also is key on the two difficult finishing holes. The 17th is a 420-yard par 4 with a pond on the right. The 18th is a monster par 4 of 464 yards along old Bunny Lake, which comes into play on the right, especially at the 12,000-square-foot bowl-shaped green that sits below the sprawling hotel.

While the Brute has lived on with some tweaking here and there, its old sidekick, the Briar Patch, is but a memory. It has been remodeled to such an extent that the original design by a couple of young designers called Dye and Nicklaus is long gone. And it has been transformed into a much more conventional layout by Bob Cupp. That's right. *The* Pete Dye and *the* Jack Nicklaus collaborated on the old Briar Patch, completed in 1971. Dye, for one, doesn't look back on the experience fondly, once griping: "That would have been a nice piece of land. Then they decided to put in an airport, a horse farm, a ski hill—all after we started the golf course. So it kind of got screwed up a little." Dye and Nicklaus later abandoned the project, and the final 14 holes were built on the cheap.

But the Milwaukee-based Marcus Corp. (known for its movie theater chain) helped rescue the resort and the old Briar Patch in the 1990s, pumping millions of dollars into updating the hotel and redoing the Briar Patch. Now, The Highlands at the Grand Geneva Resort and Spa is a fitting partner for The Brute, a classic course that has a lot of stories to tell.

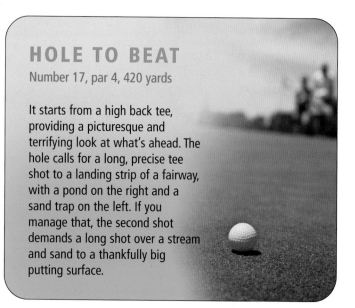

HOLE TO BEAT
Number 17, par 4, 420 yards

It starts from a high back tee, providing a picturesque and terrifying look at what's ahead. The hole calls for a long, precise tee shot to a landing strip of a fairway, with a pond on the right and a sand trap on the left. If you manage that, the second shot demands a long shot over a stream and sand to a thankfully big putting surface.

The Bull at
Pinehurst Farms

SHEBOYGAN FALLS

When the owners of Pinehurst Farms decided to break with 150 years of tradition and turn their cattle-breeding operation into a golf course, there was one thing they didn't want to part with: their pride.

If the farm's reputation for breeding national champion Holsteins was over, they wanted to make sure another championship tradition ensued. So when the Bachmann family went looking for an architect to bring their vision to life, they settled on one of golf's greatest champions, Jack Nicklaus.

The result in 2002 not only was the first Jack Nicklaus signature course in Wisconsin, but also a layout that many people call one of the best in the state, and that's saying something considering The Bull is just down the road from Pete Dye's four Kohler courses, including Whistling Straits.

THE BULL AT PINEHURST FARMS

5,087 to 7,332 yards
par 72
rating 76.4
slope 146

ARCHITECT
Jack Nicklaus

CALL
(920) 467-1500

WEB SITE
www.golfthebull.com

ADDRESS
1 Long Drive, Sheboygan Falls, WI 53085

DIRECTIONS
From the intersection of U.S. highways 28 and 32 on the south side of Sheboygan Falls, take Route 32 south to the first left.

When Nicklaus does a signature course, he puts his heart and soul into it. At The Bull, the man known as the Golden Bear made at least six trips to Sheboygan Falls to monitor every

aspect of course development with his design team. And when the course opened, he was there to play and walk all 7,300 yards of it, despite an artificial hip and other leg problems that have slowed his golf game.

His design game certainly was in championship form on the former 418-acre farm. Fortunately, this farm was more than pasture. The land includes deep ravines, wetlands, thick woods and the Onion River as it winds toward Lake Michigan. The Bachmanns hired Nicklaus because they knew he could deliver what they wanted: a championship-level course but one that didn't intimidate middle and high handicappers.

Similar to Nicklaus' Muirfield Village, which is home to his Memorial Tournament each year in Dublin, Ohio, The

Bull is charged with one memorable hole after another. There's the 432-yard fifth bending around a deep ravine and past thick woods; the 193-yard sixth over the ravine; the tight 321-yard seventh, requiring two well-placed shots; the 568-yard eighth over the Onion; the 178-yard 15th with water lapping at the green; the 422-yard 16th with the approach over a gully and through a chute of big pines; and the 485-yard par 4 18th with a tee shot over water and then uphill to the green.

The Bull's upscale facilities include a stylish clubhouse, restaurant, banquet and conference center and adjacent housing development.

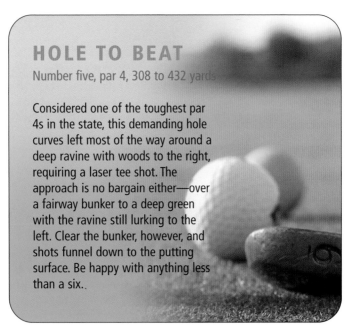

HOLE TO BEAT
Number five, par 4, 308 to 432 yards

Considered one of the toughest par 4s in the state, this demanding hole curves left most of the way around a deep ravine with woods to the right, requiring a laser tee shot. The approach is no bargain either—over a fairway bunker to a deep green with the ravine still lurking to the left. Clear the bunker, however, and shots funnel down to the putting surface. Be happy with anything less than a six.

Erin Hills

ERIN

Imagine a landscape so natural for golf that the persnickety United States Golf Association picks the site for one of its championships even before it opens.

A place so meant for golf that noted designers Hurdzan and Fry (along with Ron Whitten) only had to use major dirt-moving maneuvers on four of the 18 holes.

That is Erin Hills, a course that was awarded a U.S.G.A. event—the 2008 Women's Amateur Public Links—before it had even been seeded. Leading up to its late season opening in 2006, the course received deserved rave reviews.

Most of the credit goes to Bob Lang, a developer who saw the potential in a great tract of land northwest of greater Milwaukee and who has built a European styled hotel in nearby Delafield (the aptly named Delafield Hotel) to accommodate the traveling golfer who wants a more genuine experience.

The only thing missing is sea mist, but Erin Hills' "Sea of Fescue" envelops the course like a low-hanging fog and

ERIN HILLS

4,543 to 7,824 yards
par 72
rating 77.7
slope 141

ARCHITECTS
Michael Hurdzan and
Dana Fry with Ron Whitten

CALL
(262) 670-8600

WEB SITE
www.erinhills.com

ADDRESS
7169 County Hwy O,
Hartford, WI 53027

DIRECTIONS
Take U.S. Highway 83
north of Interstate 94 to
Country Road O, take a left
and travel 1.1 miles to golf
course entrance on left.

provides a real links experience in Wisconsin's beautiful, glacially shaped Kettle Moraines. But those lovely, waving grasses are a burial ground for golf balls. The fairways are generous, but don't miss them. As one fellow golf writer quipped after a round at Erin Hills, "Tall fescue, we learned, is Gaelic for 'kiss your golf ball goodbye.'"

The course is full of surprises—views of Holy Hill in the distance, varied bird life, stands of hardwood, greens that funnel to the hole and a variety of blind shots and hidden hazards—the kind that you find in the birthplace of golf and on old American courses built by Old World architects.

Number seven, a par 3 measuring 223 from the very tips but playing at 184 for most of us, is a blind shot. You aim for the white rock, trying to remember the green sits 30 feet below the horizon. Number 10, at 624 from the blue tees, features an opening drive uphill to a broad plateau and to a mostly hidden fairway. You can hardly see the sharply elevated and extremely sloping green from the fairway on the par 4 15th—dubbed the "Volcano" hole—but you are plenty grateful when you find your ball on the short grass atop the natural mound. Throughout the course, watch for hidden pot bunkers and mounds.

The course stretches up to a gargantuan 8,000 yards to accommodate the ever-spiraling length of the pros' games, but five sets of conventional tees provide a comfortable distance for anyone's game—whether walking or riding. Another golfer-friendly feature, at least for those from Wisconsin, is the cheaper in-state rate. But out-of-state golfers shouldn't be deterred from a golf journey to remember.

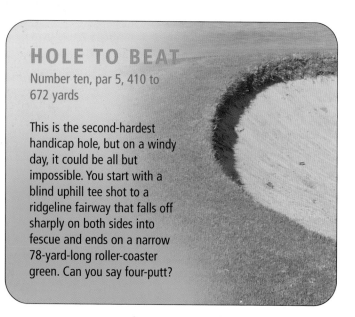

HOLE TO BEAT

Number ten, par 5, 410 to 672 yards

This is the second-hardest handicap hole, but on a windy day, it could be all but impossible. You start with a blind uphill tee shot to a ridgeline fairway that falls off sharply on both sides into fescue and ends on a narrow 78-yard-long roller-coaster green. Can you say four-putt?

The Palmer Course
at Geneva National

LAKE GENEVA

The other lake in town, lovely Lake Como, is the site of a resort featuring a trio of fine courses designed by a few familiar names: Palmer, Trevino and Player.

Play all 54 holes if you can. You'll find few disappointments among them.

If you can't, we recommend the Palmer course—Arnie's first Wisconsin layout and what pros call the toughest of the three.

The Palmer and Trevino courses opened in August 1991, with the Player course finally opening its second nine in 2000. In 1991, two of the greats were on hand for a well-publicized grand opening. Lee Trevino christened his course by shooting a six-under-par 66. The next day, Palmer played his course and shot an even-par 72. "I heard what he shot on his course, and that must be a lot easier than mine," the King quipped.

THE PALMER COURSE AT GENEVA NATIONAL

4,892 to 7,177 yards
par 72
rating 74.7
slope 140

ARCHITECT
Arnold Palmer

CALL
(262) 245-7000, ext. 520

WEB SITE
www.genevanationalresort.com

ADDRESS
1221 Geneva National South, Lake Geneva, WI 53147

DIRECTIONS
Located west of Lake Geneva, travel 4.5 miles on U.S. Highway 50.

Palmer may not have been entirely kidding. Playing his course requires length, accuracy and clear thinking. Stay out of the woods and in the fairway. And stay below the hole, because those sloping greens are trouble if you're putting downhill.

Palmer and his team made the most of a splendid tract of land, rising 300 feet above Lake Como to hilly uplands wooded with stands of hardwood. "We had some wonderful terrain at Geneva National that lent itself to building a very interesting and good, solid course," he says about his work. "It's the kind of golf course that will only get better and better."

Warm up, because the first hole is a tester. This 387-yard par 4 requires you to clear the large oak tree on the right with your drive and then avoid the creek to a severely sloping green on your approach.

The course emerges from the woods for a time on the eighth hole, a difficult par 3 of 227 yards from the long tees to a green tucked behind the corner of long pond on the right. Big sand traps discourage bailing out to the left, but they are a good target if you don't hit it too far, where out-of-bounds lurks.

Tree-lined fairways and abundant water greet you on much of the back nine. Success on the 184-yard, par 3 13th means negotiating a downhill shot to a wooded hollow, where the green is guarded by two ponds. Number 14, a 578-yard par 5, is narrow and heavily wooded all the way as it doglegs left to a green that severely slopes from front to back; favor the right side on this hole.

As Palmer says, it keeps getting better and better. Now comes hole 15, a 393-yard par 4 that Arnie dubbed "a tremendous golf hole." To the left is a wide-open fairway, which narrows quickly as it bends right around a pond and trees. Standing on the elevated tee, Palmer said "you take off just as much as your guts will let you take off."

Now come the views of Lake Como and a furious finish. Number 16, 218 yards from the back tee, is downhill with the lake appearing to back up right to a green where two bunkers guard the entrance. Number 17 sweeps around the lake shoreline for 579 yards. It's a personal favorite of Palmer's. The 18th, an uphill 435-yard par 4, provides a fitting finish with a dozen sand traps and a water hazard between you and a 19th hole respite.

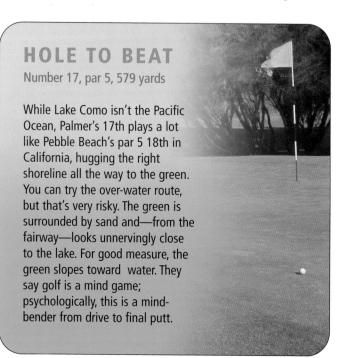

HOLE TO BEAT
Number 17, par 5, 579 yards

While Lake Como isn't the Pacific Ocean, Palmer's 17th plays a lot like Pebble Beach's par 5 18th in California, hugging the right shoreline all the way to the green. You can try the over-water route, but that's very risky. The green is surrounded by sand and—from the fairway—looks unnervingly close to the lake. For good measure, the green slopes toward water. They say golf is a mind game; psychologically, this is a mind-bender from drive to final putt.

House on the
Rock Golf Club

SPRING GREEN

Robert Trent Jones Sr. got it Wright when he designed 18 holes in a splendid little valley close to the Wisconsin River.

That's as in Frank Lloyd Wright, the architect whose world-famed Taliesin estate is just down the road.

They didn't collaborate on the golf course, but their artistic skills appear to meld on this creation. Jones once said his design "had nothing to do with Frank Lloyd Wright" but he conceded "the association was unique." Robert Graves, a former Wright associate who once managed the golf property, was more effusive. "(Jones) had everything to work with. It couldn't be more unobtrusive that it is. It's something Mr. Wright could have understood very well."

Once The Springs, it has been renamed the House on the Rock Golf Club by the owners of that big Wisconsin tourist attraction just seven miles away.

The busy, one-of-a-kind House on the Rock site and the course are worlds apart, however, especially if you're a single on a

HOUSE ON THE ROCK GOLF CLUB

5,358 to 6,597 yards
par 72
rating 71.7
slope 126

ARCHITECT
Robert Trent Jones Sr.

CALL
(800) 822-7774

WEB SITE
www.thehouseontherock.com

ADDRESS
400 Springs Drive, Spring Green, WI 53588

DIRECTIONS
Located one-half mile south of Tower Hill Road, one mile east of Highway 23 and approximately one mile east of the Frank Lloyd Wright Museum.

bluebird Wisconsin spring morning back in the neck of Jones Valley (named for Wright's uncle, not the course architect), the dew heavy on the grass, a wild turkey pecking at the edge of the woods. In the neck of the valley are two difficult holes: the 13th (a long par 4 uphill and doglegging around woods) and the 14th (a downhill par 5 with a wooded hillside left, trees on the right and water at the long, narrow green).

Preceding those two holes is a par 5 said to be Jones' favorite hole on the course. The hole, a dogleg right, allows big hitters to go for the big two-tiered green (the largest on the course) in two if they want to risk hitting into large sand traps front and left and water right.

Number two is a favorite 203-yard par 3 over water to a shallow, shaded green. Number 11 is another pretty par 3, but much shorter, where golfers hit from an elevated tee to a long green guarded by a pond on the right side.

For years after its opening in the mid-1960s under former Johnson Wax executive Willard "Bud" Keland, golfers would pay low green fees at a pro shop house in a trailer near the first tee. Dreams of a big resort were hard to realize because Spring Green always seemed a little too much out of the way and financing was scarce.

But the resort finally was built, and the place has been discovered. In fact, Democratic presidential candidate John Kerry secluded himself and his team at the resort to prepare for debates with George Bush in 2004.

So no longer can you play a Trent Jones creation at bargain basement prices. On the other hand, now there's a resort with full amenities and an Andy North/Roger Packard-designed nine-hole course that opened in 1994. The outdoor American Players Theater is adjacent to the golf property, and Tower Hill State Park sits near the course entrance, not far from the Wisconsin River.

Some changes to Jones' design have been made over the years—a very un-Jones-like moat was inserted on the third hole, for example. But his initial design remains relatively intact—in harmony with the land and the architectural philosophy of Frank Lloyd Wright.

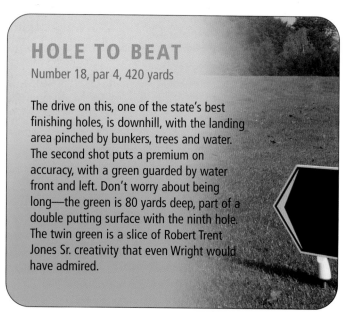

HOLE TO BEAT
Number 18, par 4, 420 yards

The drive on this, one of the state's best finishing holes, is downhill, with the landing area pinched by bunkers, trees and water. The second shot puts a premium on accuracy, with a green guarded by water front and left. Don't worry about being long—the green is 80 yards deep, part of a double putting surface with the ninth hole. The twin green is a slice of Robert Trent Jones Sr. creativity that even Wright would have admired.

Lake Arrowhead
Golf Club
NEKOOSA

Golfers may think they're seeing a vision when they visit secluded Lake Arrowhead, 36 holes of golf weaving through pine-studded forests and past sparkling ponds in the sandy barrens of central Wisconsin.

Lake Arrowhead, named for a nearby lake, was little more than a developer's dream—one that didn't take off immediately—in the late 1970s. Beset by financial problems and slow housing sales early on, Lake Arrowhead initially was a nine-hole course, opening in 1982, three years after construction began. What now is known as the Pines course was finished with a second nine in 1985.

When people began to discover the beauty of the area and the course, it took off. In 1998, the Lakes course was added.

Although it took nearly 20 years to complete, Lake

LAKE ARROWHEAD GOLF CLUB

Pines course
5,213 to 6,624 yards
par 72
rating 72.1
slope 132

ARCHITECT
Ken Killian and Dick Nugent

Lakes course
5,272 to 7,105 yards
par 72
rating 74.8
slope 140

ARCHITECT
Ken Killian

CALL
(715) 325-2929

WEB SITE
www.lakearrowheadgolf.com

ADDRESS
1195 Apache Lane, Nekoosa, WI 54457

DIRECTIONS
Located 13 miles south of Wisconsin Rapids on U.S. Highway 13; 35 miles north of Wisconsin Dells.

Arrowhead, which looks and feels a bit like famous Pinehurst in the sand-hill region of North Carolina, has proved worth the wait. Golfers can choose from two championship-style courses with lush fairways, large, undulating greens, sculpted bunkers and plenty of trees and water to shape the holes. Homeowners have added amenities at the complex: two pools, a beach, tennis courts and discounted green fees.

A perfect day at Lake Arrowhead would be 18 in the morning, lunch at one of the two clubhouses, a three-mile drive to the other course and 18 in the afternoon. And some birdies.

The Pines course, despite the housing development, still feels secluded as it winds through 130 acres of pine and oak trees, over a pond on the par 3 fourth hole and around a small lake dividing the par 5 ninth and par 4 10th holes. Trees and natural sandy waste areas are common throughout the course, but water comes into play often, including the par 5 16th and par 3 17th holes. The Pines finishes with a 460-yard par 4 past a 55-yard-long fairway bunker to a two-tiered green.

Eight little lakes, along with more oaks, pines and big waste areas, dot the Lakes course, which is about 500 yards longer and eight slope points higher than the Pines. The signature hole may be number three, a 174-yard shot over a broad pond with a waterfall behind the green. Holes 12 and 18 each have two ponds. The 18th is a double-dogleg, 448-yard par 4 with water left and right. A par would be the perfect way to end a day at Lake Arrowhead.

HOLE TO BEAT

Pines Course, number nine, par 5, 455 to 516 yards

Big hitters can reach this green in two, if they can drive it through trees close to 300 yards to the lake's edge and then carry the lake and a beach bunker. The conservative approach is to lay up right, where the hole doglegs around the pond, pitch it in and hope for a one-putt birdie.

The Links at
Lawsonia

GREEN LAKE

Big Chicago money built one of the best courses in the state. And the Depression, World War II gas rationing and military expansion almost ruined it.

But the venerable Links course at Lawsonia has survived decades to delight visiting golfers. It opened in 1930 on a fine design by William Langford and Theodore Moreau. They traveled to Great Britain to sketch and photograph famous holes at other links and then laid out a course with multitiered greens, some 90 bunkers and deep rough atop a windswept plateau above Green Lake, Wisconsin's deepest at 237 feet.

Lawsonia began back in 1887 when Jessie Lawson, wife of *Chicago Daily News* founder Victor Lawson, took a pleasure cruise on the western end of Green Lake. A storm forced her and her chums to shore, where they sought shelter on a secluded spot shaded by a single tree. Jessie talked her husband into buying the first 10 acres of what was to become the 1,100-acre Lone Tree Farm.

THE LINKS AT LAWSONIA

5,078 to 6,801 yards
par 73
rating 73
slope 130

ARCHITECTS
William Langford and Theodore Moreau

CALL
(800) 529-4453

WEB SITE
www.lawsonia.com

ADDRESS
W2615 S. Valley View Drive, Green Lake, WI 54941

DIRECTIONS
Entrance is two miles west of Green Lake on U.S. Highway 23.

Some $8 million later, the Lawsons had an elaborate estate that included Italian-tiled boathouses, formal gardens, seven water towers (including the 200-foot Judson Tower where Jessie entertained guests for tea at the top), a little nine-hole course (now gone) and the largest barn in Wisconsin

(once housing prized Jerseys, now a giant maintenance building). Mrs. Lawson died in 1914, Mr. Lawson died in 1925 and then the H.O. Stone Co. of Chicago bought the estate. The new owners invested another $3 million, developing exclusive homes, the Lawsonia Country Club hotel and casino plus the Links course (cost: $250,000).

The course later hosted the Little Lawsonia Open, which drew names such as Ben Hogan, Sam Snead and Byron Nelson; Nelson shot a 69 here in 1939, then a course record.

But the development went bust, leaving the mortgage-holding bank to operate it for about 10 years. The Depression, and then World War II gas rationing finally closed the resort for two years in the early 1940s, and the U.S. government once considered buying it as the site for the Air Force Academy. Instead the men in blue went west, and the government leased the giant barn along the front nine to house about 450 German POWs. Things got so bad that in 1944, the front nine of the Links course served as a cow pasture.

The Northern Baptist Convention bought the property for a mere $300,000 in 1943 and has brought the course back over time. Today the course and a conference center are managed by the succeeding American Baptist Assembly as a "place for renewal." That's appropriate, considering the addition of the Woodlands course (opened a nine at a time in 1983 and 1991) and the 2000 architectural restoration of the old Links course. Fairways have been widened, trees removed and steep bunkers restored so it plays more like the way it did when the golf greats were on the scene. Renew your love for the way golf used to be played at Lawsonia.

HOLE TO BEAT
Number seven, par 3, 161 yards

The seventh at Lawsonia Links isn't long. There isn't any water. No sand. No trees. What's so hard about it? Some people say it's the boxcar that's supposedly buried beneath the green. That boxcar—or whatever it is—forms a nearly vertical front wall on the green. From below, it looks like the Green Monster in left field at Boston's Fenway Park. A chip from the base of the seventh green is like trying to hit up an elevator shaft and hold the shot on the second floor.

Madeline Island
Golf Club

LA POINTE

The first drive at Madeline Island Golf Club is hard to beat: Steer your vehicle onto the ferry at Bayfield, head to the observation deck, fill your lungs with some of the freshest air around and enjoy the views of Lake Superior. Relaxed yet?

Madeline Island Golf Club isn't one of the best-known public golf courses in Wisconsin, but situated as it is in Lake Superior, it arguably is the best setting for golf in the state. The island, one of the 22 Apostle Islands, is known more for its breathtaking beauty, museum, trails and parks than it is for golf, but don't underestimate the golf.

Designed by master architect Robert Trent Jones Sr., with help from his son, budding architect Robert Trent Jones Jr., the course has been part of summer vacations on the island since it opened in 1968. Original owner Theodore Gary, one of the island's summer residents, spent $4 million on the

MADELINE ISLAND GOLF CLUB

5,506 to 6,366 yards
par 71
rating 71
slope 131

ARCHITECT
Robert Trent Jones Sr.

CALL
(715) 747-3212

WEB SITE
www.madelineislandgolf.com

ADDRESS
498 Old Fort Road,
La Pointe, WI 54850

DIRECTIONS
Take the 15-minute ferry ride from Bayfield to Madeline Island. From the ferry dock, turn right on Main Street and follow it approximately one mile to Old Fort Road. The course is across from the Yacht Club.

course, including three years of clearing the rocky land and ferrying topsoil to the island.

Like the ride to the island, the course is memorable. It's only a nine-hole layout, but it's designed to play like 18. The second time around, golfers can play separate back-nine tees, fairways and pins that are adjacent to the front-nine holes. Seven of the double greens have two pins, one for the front and one for the back nine.

For example, the first hole is 399 yards to a pin on the right; as number 10, it's 444 yards to a different pin on the left side of the green. The second hole is 109 yards to the left green area; as number 11 it's 181 yards to a pin on the right and over more of the pond that separates the tees and green. Several holes have separate front-back fairways. Suffice to say, check the scorecard before heading to a tee or taking aim at a fairway or flagstick.

The course, partly open and partly wooded, plays tougher than its 6,366 yards because of elevation changes, the cool, unpredictable climate and lengthy par 4s. Holes 10 through 12, including two long par 4s and a par 3 over water, are considered the toughest stretch on the course.

With many recreational opportunities on the island, the golf course often isn't full and the pace is laid back. If the ferry is running late and you miss your tee time, don't worry. Course management is used to it. The weather can change by the hour, so bring a sweater.

And after you swing, don't forget to look up and enjoy the views—and the drive back to the mainland.

HOLE TO BEAT

Number nine par 3, 79 to 179 yards

Steeply downhill, this fun finishing hole offers a view of Lake Superior and a challenge: Get the distance right to this shallow green or pay the price. Short is in a pond and long is in a sand trap.

Mascoutin Golf Club

BERLIN

Three centuries ago, a tribe of fire-worshipping Native Americans called the Mascoutin lived in and around this part of the Fox River Valley. Nowadays, the worshipping often is for 27 holes of golf off the beaten path but not to be missed.

Welcome to Mascoutin Golf Club, where the father-and-son team of Lawrence and Roger Packard, familiar names in Wisconsin golf history, crafted a state classic that opened in 1975. Rick Jacobson, who studied under Lawrence Packard and Jack Nicklaus and whose name is affixed to a growing number of state courses, added his own nine holes in 1999.

Together their works comprise one of the best golf venues in Wisconsin—a great slice of small-town living (Berlin, home to many stately Victorian homes, is also Wisconsin's "fur and leather capital"), the state's fine inland scenery and the work of the Packards.

The elder Packard's public

MASCOUTIN GOLF CLUB

5,124 to 6,893 yards
par 72
rating 73.2
slope 132

ARCHITECTS
Lawrence and Roger Packard, original 18

CALL
(920) 361-2360

WEB SITE
www.mascoutingolf.com

ADDRESS
W1635 County Road A, Berlin, WI 54923

DIRECTIONS
From Milwaukee, take U.S. Highway 41 north to Fond du Lac, then travel west on Route 23 to Green Lake. From there, take Route 49 north, and then a left on County Road A. From Madison, take U.S. Highway 151 north to Route 73, and continue north on Route 23. From there, travel east on Route 49, and north to County Road A.

course design work includes: Brown County Golf Course near Green Bay, Naga-Waukee Golf Course in Pewaukee and Peninsula State Park Golf Course in Door County. Son Roger's résumé includes Timber Ridge in Minocqua, Trappers Turn and the newer North Nine at House on the Rock (the latter two with two-time U.S. Open champion Andy North of Madison).

The Jacobson nine (the Blue nine) is a fun track with creative designing. The cliff hole, a nifty 393-yard par 4, starts in a wooded chute to a tiered fairway that slopes right to left. The second shot is abruptly downhill to a green flanked by trees and large waste bunkers on the left and front and a carved-out cliff on the right side.

The original layout (now the Red and White nines) is the one that hosts most tournaments, and it's the one that has matured into a course that will test just about anyone's game. Course managers augmented the Packards' design on 220 acres of hilly land overlooking the Fox River with an aggressive tree-planting program that has paid dividends 20 years later. The course, already tough with big, slick, rolling greens and spacious traps (some 65 traps in all), has tightened considerably over the years. And the course was selectively lengthened in preparation for the 105th Wisconsin State Amateur Championship in 2006 with new tees on number two (now a par 5 of 543 yards) and number 10 (now a par 4 of 428 yards).

When tournament directors let the rough grow and let the greens get super fast, the competitive cream rises to the top. The rest of us just try to keep our iron shots below the hole so we're always putting uphill.

If that isn't enough, Mascoutin grips your attention on the closing four holes, each of which feature major water hazards. The 412-yard par 4, number six on the White nine, requires you to hit from an elevated tee to a 25-yard-wide landing area with out-of-bounds left and a pond on the right. The next hole is a long par 5 of 552 yards, with a double turn to the left around a tall and wide oak on the left; the pond and trees on right leave little room for bailing out. The 183-yard par 3 requires a shot to a trap-protected green with a hard back-to-front slope and water along the right side.

And then you're faced with one of the best finishing holes in the state, one that will decide many a match. The 384-yard hole has more of the water, trees, sand and green contours that make Mascoutin a must visit.

HOLE TO BEAT
Number 18, par 4, 384 yards

Trouble seems to lurk everywhere on this hole. The drive is troublesome because woods on the left and a big tree on the right pinch the fairway about 150 yards out from the green. Pros like to try to hit past that tree with a driver or 3-wood. The approach is over a pond to a green shaded on the left by a big oak growing from a bunker that protects the front of the green. This is one of the state's best finishing holes.

Northern Bay
Golf Resort

ARKDALE

Developers at Northern Bay have gone to great lengths to draw tourists and vacationers to their site, spending $150 million with an 18-hole golf course, a marina on big Castle Rock Lake, condominiums, home sites and eventually a lodge with an indoor water park, restaurant and spa.

The golf course might have been enough. Built on rolling, sandy, tree-lined central Wisconsin terrain, it has more than enough good holes to keep golfers coming back. And that's not counting the replica holes, seven of which duplicate famous holes from across the country. Give credit to the developers: Some of the nonreplica holes are just as good. They didn't completely hang their hat on someone else's ideas.

If you like greatest hits albums, you'll love parts of Northern Bay. There's the island par 3 17th from the Tournament Players Course (the 10th at Northern Bay), the par 5 13th from Augusta National (11th at Northern Bay) and

NORTHERN BAY GOLF RESORT

5,197 to 7,223 yards
par 72
rating 74.4
slope 131

CALL
(800) 350-0049

WEB SITE
www.northernbayresort.com

ADDRESS
1844 20th Ave., Arkdale, WI 54613

DIRECTIONS
Take Interstate 90-94 to County Road HH (exit 79). Take HH to Highway 82, then turn right over the Wisconsin River bridge, then left onto County Z for 14 miles. Turn left on Dakota Avenue and proceed one mile to the course entrance.

the par 4 18th at Bay Hill (18th at Northern Bay), all of which look and play very similar to the originals—in other words, tough.

The course goes to great lengths to reproduce the holes. The island hole has vertical railroad ties framing the island; Rae's Creek meanders in front of the 11th; and boulders line the pond that guards the 18th, all features on the originals. The third hole at Northern Bay is a replica of Number 16 at Augusta. One word of caution: Stay below the cup on this slippery green.

Other Northern Bay cutouts replicate holes from Firestone, Oakland Hills and Oakmont. Signs at the tee designate each replica hole.

Whether or not you recognize the replica hole—the big pine trees are missing, for example, on the Augusta National 11th—or care, you still get to play a great golf hole.

The replicas, combined with the originals, form a memorable and challenging 7,223-yard layout that has a little bit of everything. Golfers will play many original holes—the double dogleg, 543-yard eighth hole; the narrow, downhill 13th, 401 yards; or the picturesque 641-yard 15th—and forget all about Oakmont's church pew bunker they just passed.

Northern Bay features water on six holes and about 80 bunkers, including one that's about 250 yards long, lining the right side of the first fairway. While the first three holes skirt resort development areas, the par 72 course, about a half-hour drive north of Wisconsin Dells, pulls away into the woods that help make Northern Bay a course to remember.

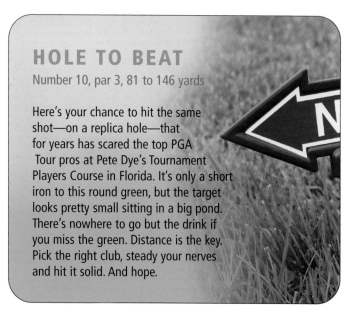

HOLE TO BEAT
Number 10, par 3, 81 to 146 yards

Here's your chance to hit the same shot—on a replica hole—that for years has scared the top PGA Tour pros at Pete Dye's Tournament Players Course in Florida. It's only a short iron to this round green, but the target looks pretty small sitting in a big pond. There's nowhere to go but the drink if you miss the green. Distance is the key. Pick the right club, steady your nerves and hit it solid. And hope.

Northwood
Golf Club
RHINELANDER

In Wisconsin, when people refer to the legends of the north woods, they usually are talking about the big fish that got away, the 30-point buck, Paul Bunyan or some other tall tale.

When it comes to golf up north, Wisconsin has something more than a rural legend: It has Northwood Golf Club near Rhinelander, an 18-hole beauty that lives up to its name as a symbol of the state's famous north country. Cut from stands of donated Wausau Paper Company forest, it's as real as the Titleists that rattle off its tree limbs.

The course was a bit of a pipe dream for the city of Rhinelander, which had mulled the idea for 20 years. In the 1980s, the city finally secured the land and hired Minneapolis architect Don Herfort to extract 18 holes from an 800-acre tract. The result was a course that looked natural and played fair when it opened in 1989. It has continued to improve with updated cart paths, two new lakes and other renovations in the early 2000s.

Northwood may be beautiful, but it bites: Few courses up north will eat more golf balls. The fairways have wide landing

NORTHWOOD GOLF CLUB

5,338 to 6,724 yards
par 72
rating 73.2
slope 137

ARCHITECT
Don Herfort

ADDRESS
3131 Golf Course Road,
Rhinelander, WI 54501

CALL
(715) 282-6565

WEB SITE
www.northwoodgolfclub.com

DIRECTIONS
Three miles west of
Rhinelander on Route 8.

areas, and the greens are large, but off-line often is off the course at Northwood. Because Herfort left thick woods bordering most fairways, balls that go in the woods stay there or, if found, result in unplayable lies.

How can Northwood be tamed? A little forest at a time. It's a classic position course requiring well-placed tee shots and patience. If you can't hit straight, it could be a long day. Play for position on the par 5s and keep the driver in the bag on the shorter par 4s.

The front nine is the hilliest at Northwood, but it sets up nicely with many downhill tee shots or approaches. A good example is number four, a pretty 402-yard par 4 that descends a hill. The approach is to a green jutting from a hillside with a pond lurking on the left. The fifth also is a downhill par 4, 366 yards, with the green nestled in a bowl of trees around a corner.

The back nine is more scenic than the front, mostly because of a bog that was dredged to make a finger lake. The bog creeps into play on holes 11, 12 and 17.

Along with the signature hole, the par 4 17th, a dogleg carry over a pond, a hole to watch for on the back is number 16, a 527-yard par 5. From a hilltop tee, golfers can see the green a quarter-mile straight ahead. But it's an obstacle course to the finish. Trees line the first 300 yards of the chute-like fairway. Then golfers must decide whether to attempt to clear a 30-yard-wide pond on their second shot or play right of it. The green is tucked into more trees, the key element that makes Northwood a classic up north course.

HOLE TO BEAT
Number 17, par 4, 300 to 400 yards

Two solid shots are required here. The first order of business is a straight tee shot. Steer right of the pond—it may not be visible down the left side— through trees to the corner of the dogleg. Then, steady your nerves for an all-carry short-to-middle iron over the pond to a wide green.

The Orchards
at Egg Harbor

EGG HARBOR

Many people who visit Door County never get to the inland part of the peninsula that juts out into Lake Michigan.

They don't know what they're missing.

While the inland, mostly agricultural part of the Door Peninsula lacks the spectacular water views seen along the coasts, the hilly, wooded and farmed area is a pleasantly quiet complement to the summer hustle and bustle on the Green Bay side of Door County.

And here, near Egg Harbor, you'll find a championship course unlike most of the short resort courses in this prime Wisconsin vacationland. The Orchards at Egg Harbor lives up to its name, running through ample acres of working orchards, stands of birch, maples and evergreens, and past meadows and a five-acre man-made lake.

William Newcomb, an Ann Arbor, Michigan, designer, and the developers made the most of this prime real estate, even leaving enough room for a comfortable clubhouse and a

THE ORCHARDS AT EGG HARBOR

5,530 to 7,206 yards
par 72
rating 75
slope 131

ARCHITECT
William Newcomb

CALL
(920) 868-2483

WEB SITE
www.orchardsateggharbor.com

ADDRESS
8125 Heritage Lake Road,
Egg Harbor, WI 54209

DIRECTIONS
Located north of Egg Harbor off U.S. Highway 42. Turn right on County Road EE, then right on Heritage Lake Road.

driving range. Newcomb, who used to work with Pete Dye, also has designed some notable courses on the other side of the big pond—including tracks at the Boyne Highlands and Grand Traverse resorts.

A variety of tee boxes accommodate the low- and high-handicappers, but this is not the kind of course for the once-a-year vacation golfer. Door County offers plenty of other golfing options and details can be found at www.doorcountygolf.com.

At the Orchards, you must mind your game to score well because hazards and woods will swallow up your bad shots. Add in some wind, and big numbers likely will occur.

That wind could play the most havoc when playing the trio of finishing holes around the manmade lake. Number 16 is a straightaway 577-yard par 5 where water on the right comes into play on the approach. Number 17 is a picture-perfect par 3 of 195 yards with water at the green. And number 18 is a 550-yard par 5 that starts from elevated tees and requires a booming drive over water to set yourself up for par or birdie; the fairway narrows dramatically from there with sand along the left side and then more sand at the green.

For splendid water views courtesy of Mother Nature, visit Peninsula State Park Golf Course in nearby Ephraim. This 6,308-yard, par 71 course, once redesigned by Lawrence Packard, is a longtime favorite of Door County visitors who love to play old number eight. Packard, who spent an occasional summer vacation in Door, had the good sense to keep intact this tiny par 3.

Players love to talk about how they handled the trademark 69-yard shot over a 50-foot cliff toward a 30-foot-high totem pole marking the grave site of Potawatomi Chief Simon Kahquados.

The only state park golf course first opened in 1921 as a six-holer. Peninsula offers splendid views of Eagle Harbor and Ephraim from several holes, especially the downhill par 3 17th. Call (920) 854-5791 or visit www.peninsulagolf.org.

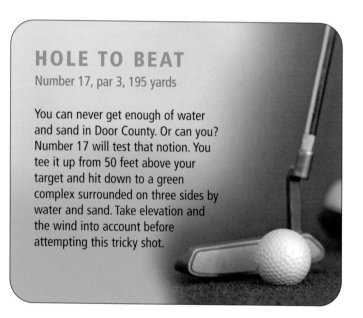

HOLE TO BEAT
Number 17, par 3, 195 yards

You can never get enough of water and sand in Door County. Or can you? Number 17 will test that notion. You tee it up from 50 feet above your target and hit down to a green complex surrounded on three sides by water and sand. Take elevation and the wind into account before attempting this tricky shot.

SentryWorld
STEVENS POINT

Designer Robert Trent Jones Jr. once called this course "very possibly my Mona Lisa." Indeed, could Leonardo da Vinci have painted a prettier golf hole than the par 3 16th "flower hole," with 45,000 blooming plants?

But there's so much more to SentryWorld, which opened in June 1982 to much hoopla thanks to course founder John W. Joanis, then president of Sentry Insurance Co. The globetrotting 14-handicapper was the man behind transforming 270 acres of swamp and woodland into a multimillion-dollar golf course and sports complex enjoyed by employees and visitors alike.

SentryWorld was Joanis' baby, his attempt to buy instant tradition and publicity for his company and his town. SentryWorld never got the big time pro tournament he dreamed of

SENTRYWORLD

5,108 to 6,951 yards
par 72
rating 74.4
slope 142

ARCHITECT
Robert Trent Jones Jr.

CALL
(866) 479-6753

WEB SITE
www.sentryworld.com

ADDRESS
601 Michigan Avenue
N., Stevens Point, WI
54481

DIRECTIONS
Take exit 161 off
Interstate 39, turn left at
Sentry Insurance building
on the east side of
Business Highway 51
soon after the exit.

(the flower hole was his idea, meant for the TV broadcast). But the course did put the college town of Stevens Point in central Wisconsin on the map for traveling golfers. Former Wisconsin

Gov. Lee Sherman Dreyfus, who worked briefly at Sentry after leaving the governor's office at the end of 1982, once said of his friend: "It's the kind of course God would have created—had He had the money."

And thanks to Sentry, the course has been maintained and nurtured so it still ranks in the echelon of Wisconsin's best courses.

Playing SentryWorld is like playing in a well-kept arboretum where deer, geese and other wildlife abound. Flowers mix with stands of birch, pine and hardwoods amid groups of granite boulders blasted free during construction.

Water is everywhere, and Jones used the 35 acres of open water to perfection. The main lake and a connecting stream come into play on five holes—numbers three, four, five, 12 and 13. Augmenting the water hazards are some 80 sand traps and lots of trees. Number 13 is a good example of the water, sand and woods combo. The 395-yard par 4 is a 90-degree dogleg right around trees and sand that some big hitters might try to cut were it not for the water that lurks on the other side of the sloping, narrow fairway.

The finishing holes typify Jones' artistic creation. After the 173-yard flower hole, comes number 17, a testy tree-lined, downhill dogleg right of 412 yards that tempts the big driver into trouble. Resist the temptation and hit to the corner of the dogleg with an iron. At least then you'll have a chance for par if you can manage the downhill approach to a narrow opening flanked by water and trees.

The finale is a 448-yard uphill par 4 to an elevated, sloping green that will leave you gasping. The dogleg left starts out of a chute of trees over a streamlet. The hole becomes progressively more open, but then sand takes the place of trees.

Nine traps, four at the green, populate this hole. Number 18 completes a central Wisconsin golf masterpiece.

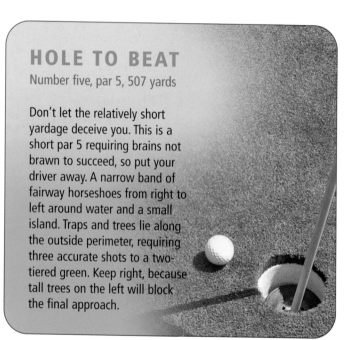

HOLE TO BEAT
Number five, par 5, 507 yards

Don't let the relatively short yardage deceive you. This is a short par 5 requiring brains not brawn to succeed, so put your driver away. A narrow band of fairway horseshoes from right to left around water and a small island. Traps and trees lie along the outside perimeter, requiring three accurate shots to a two-tiered green. Keep right, because tall trees on the left will block the final approach.

Trappers Turn
WISCONSIN DELLS

For many years, when someone mentioned golf and Wisconsin Dells in the same breath, they likely were talking about miniature or goofy golf. The Dells, with its dozens of fake grass obstacle courses, is considered the faux golf capital of the world, not to mention the water park and other self-proclaimed capitals of the world.

When two-time U.S. Open champion Andy North and architect Roger Packard unveiled Trappers Turn golf course in 1991, real golfers started taking the Dells seriously. Soon, other upscale courses followed and Wisconsin Dells became known, at least in golf circles, for more than water slides and neon-lit attractions.

Trappers Turn is the real thing. It uses the rolling, postglacial Dells landscape, which is what first drew tourists to the region in the mid-1800s, to create a memorable course. Although it's not far off Interstate 94, Trappers is near

TRAPPERS TURN

Lakes and Canyon
5,021 to 6,995 yards
par 72
rating 73.4
slope 136

Arbor
2,516 to 3,405 yards
par 36

ARCHITECTS
Andy North and Roger Packard

CALL
(800) 221-8876

WEB SITE
www.trappersturn.com

ADDRESS
652 Trappers Turn Drive, P.O. Box 176, Wisconsin Dells, WI 53965

DIRECTIONS
Take exit 85 off Interstate 90-94. Head east on U.S. Highway 12/16, then left to the course.

the Wisconsin
River and has
plenty of the
escape-to-
Wisconsin feel that
vacationers seek.

After some
renovation, the
original 18 was
stretched 500
yards to more than
6,800 and is
considered one of
the state's marquee
courses, hosting
the 1998 State Open. North's and Packard's ability to
incorporate a variety of design features is one reason golfers
keep coming back. About three-fourths of Trappers golfers
travel more than an hour to play the course.

With links-style bunkering and mounds, woods, lakes and
streams, and a Southern-style clubhouse for post-round
ruminations, it's worth the trip.

The opening nine, Lakes, winds around 17-acre Mystic
Lake. Among the best holes are number five, a 344-yarder that
demands a well-placed tee shot between two ponds, and
number nine, a 507-yard par 5 with a lake bordering the right
side and a stream cutting in front of the green.

The Canyon, or back nine, gets its name from number
seven, a 158-yard par 3 that slides downhill between rock
outcroppings into a hollow or small canyon. The nine starts
with a dogleg par 4 around trees and twice over a creek. It ends
with a 549-yard par 5 that runs sharply downhill past a

sentinel pine tree and over a creek.

In 2000, North, a Madison native and TV golf analyst, and Packard added a third nine, the Arbor. It's a 3,400-yard, par 36 course that meshes with the original 18 by offering a variety of looks and challenges. The Arbor starts on a ridge overlooking Rocky Arbor State Park. It plays past sandstone walls, has sharp elevation changes, pot bunkers, a par 3 peninsula green and a par 5 with a church pew-style bunker.

HOLE TO BEAT
Number 18, par 5, 446 to 549 yards

Steer past the big pine on the left and right fairway bunker on the downhill tee shot. The key shot is the second. Golfers must decide if they can carry a stream that runs diagonally across the fairway. The best play is down the right side, taking part of the creek out of play and setting up a clear approach to the green.

Troy Burne
Golf Club

HUDSON

The St. Croix River Valley, a steep, forested vein on Wisconsin's west-central border, always has been known for its beauty and quaint cities. It has been called Little New England and the Rhine Valley of America.

In recent years, it has become known for something else: great golf. The St. Croix Valley Golf Trail has about 15 courses and more than 250 holes, half of them new since 1990.

One course, however, and its many good holes essentially put the valley on the destination golf map: Troy Burne. When it opened in May of 1999, Troy Burne not only was immediately recognized as one of Wisconsin's best public courses but also as one of the best layouts in the Twin Cities metro area.

It all started in 1996, when PGA Tour star Tom Lehman won the British Open at Royal Lytham in England. That fall, Lehman and architects Michael Hurdzan and Dana Fry of

TROY BURNE GOLF CLUB

4,932 to 7,032 yards
par 71
rating 74.3
slope 136

ARCHITECTS
Michael Hurdzan and Dana Fry, with Tom Lehman

CALL
(877) 888-8633

WEB SITE
www.troyburne.com

ADDRESS
295 Lindsay Road, Hudson, WI 54016

DIRECTIONS
From Interstate 94 in Hudson, take exit 2 at Carmichael Road and County Road F. Turn south onto F and travel for five miles south. Troy Burne is on the right.

Cleveland, Ohio, began designing Troy Burne. The course's British imprint can be seen in amber prairie grasses framing an otherwise open landscape, 121 sand bunkers and a traditional stacked sod wall guarding a hellish pot bunker, a feature common on old-country courses. The only thing missing is an ocean.

"Our goal in building Troy Burne was to blend this region's natural beauty and characteristics into our design with as little disruption to the natural habitat as possible," said Lehman, who grew up in Austin, Minnesota, attended the University of Minnesota and played some amateur tournaments in western Wisconsin. "I expect it to be one of the best courses around, private or public, in the Midwest or anywhere else."

Troy Burne opened after more than 1 million cubic yards of dirt were moved to turn a flat farm field into a rolling acreage with several ponds and a stream. The front and back nines circle a prairie-style one-story clubhouse, which features some of Lehman's memorabilia.

Troy Burne has several distinctive holes on the front side, including a 600-yard par 5 to open play, a tough par 4 over water and a short par 4, 355 yards, pinched by 11 bunkers.

The course really takes off on holes 10 through 15, the start of "one of the best nines I've ever seen," said Bill Linneman, who rated the course for the Wisconsin State Golf

Association. Water is a factor on seven holes on the inward nine.

Highlights include: the 11th, a pretty, 176-yard downhill par 3 framed by the bubbling burne; the 483-yard 12th, a fun risk-reward par 5 with a peninsula green; the 617-yard 16th with two pot bunkers guarding the green; the picturesque 17th, 445 yards sweeping around a pond; and the 470-yard 18th, a brute atop a windswept ridge. The 18th is a demanding type of par 4 often seen at the end of a major golf tournament, something Lehman knows a little about.

Troy Burne, which has an adjacent housing development, held a Nationwide Tour event in 2004 and 2005.

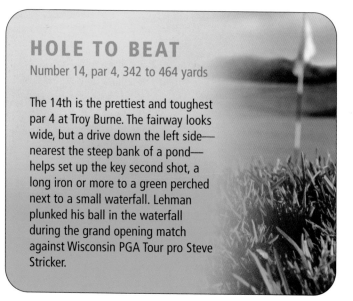

HOLE TO BEAT
Number 14, par 4, 342 to 464 yards

The 14th is the prettiest and toughest par 4 at Troy Burne. The fairway looks wide, but a drive down the left side—nearest the steep bank of a pond—helps set up the key second shot, a long iron or more to a green perched next to a small waterfall. Lehman plunked his ball in the waterfall during the grand opening match against Wisconsin PGA Tour pro Steve Stricker.

Turtleback Golf,
Dining and
Conference Center

RICE LAKE

When golf course superintendent Todd Severud and the previous owner of the Rice Lake Golf Course decided to renovate their old nine-hole layout in the early 1980s, they first took note of where they were: in a city of 8,300 in northwestern Wisconsin, a long way from major metropolitan areas. To get people to come to their course, it would have to be something special.

A teacher by trade, Severud took an independent crash course on golf design before digging in. He went with a style that was a bit o' Scotland and a bit o' Severud, choosing grass mounds and bunkers and a sprinkling of big sand traps as key features. The mounds are so prominent on some holes that the course was named after them.

"I liked the style with a lot of mounding and a lot less sand. Grass is a hazard, and the mounds are a hazard," says Severud, who remains the superintendent. "There's a Scottish

---

TURTLEBACK GOLF, DINING AND CONFERENCE CENTER

5,163 to 6,604 yards
par 71
rating 72.0
slope 130

ARCHITECT
Todd Severud

CALL
(715) 234-7641 or
(888) 300-9443

WEB SITE
www.turtlebackgolf.com

ADDRESS
West Allen Road, P.O. Box 363, Rice Lake, WI 54868

DIRECTIONS
Take Highway 53 to exit 143, travel west on Highway 48 and take a left on 19th Street and then a right on Allen Street to the course entrance.

flavor, but there's also trees. It's not a links course."

In 1985, nine new holes opened, and in 1994 a second nine was ready, eliminating the quirky old course altogether. Along with a restaurant and conference center, Turtleback became the destination facility once envisioned.

The mostly open, par 35 front nine is the shortest and easiest, but on mostly level ground it plays all of that, including a 545-yard par 5 that often is into the wind and two risk-reward par 4s that could result in birdie—or much worse.

The terrain is more varied on the back nine. The 12th hole, for example, is a 398-yard par 4 with a big fairway and room to cut the dogleg left corner. However, rows of tall red pines pinch the opening to the narrow, elevated green, necessitating a well-placed drive.

Holes 14 through 18 will test most every shot in your bag. On the par 5 14th, avoid the mounds on the drive and a gauntlet of trees on the second shot. A pond lurking behind the green forms an intimidating hazard on the 175-yard 15th hole. With the pond on the right side of the picturesque 15th, it plays much like a mirror image of the famed 16th at Augusta National, home of the Masters Tournament.

Drive it straight on the tree-lined 16th and you'll make par or better. The 17th is a brutish 454-yard par 4.

Turtleback's 18th is such a pretty and strategic hole that you'll want to play it again and again—or watch others play it from the clubhouse above the green. The hole sweeps right around a broad pond, which comes into play on the drive and second shot. Golfers can cut off some of the hole's 530 yards by going for the green in two over the pond to a well-bunkered green. "A lot of people try it, but they never find their golf ball," Severud says.

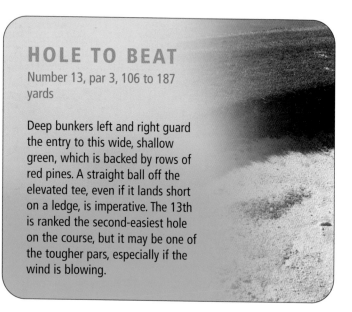

HOLE TO BEAT
Number 13, par 3, 106 to 187 yards

Deep bunkers left and right guard the entry to this wide, shallow green, which is backed by rows of red pines. A straight ball off the elevated tee, even if it lands short on a ledge, is imperative. The 13th is ranked the second-easiest hole on the course, but it may be one of the tougher pars, especially if the wind is blowing.

University Ridge
VERONA

The University of Wisconsin took decades to build its golf course, but it was worth the wait. In fact, golfers at University Ridge, about 13 miles west of the UW–Madison campus in downtown Madison, get to play two courses, in a sense.

That's because the Robert Trent Jones Jr.-designed 18, opened in 1991 at a cost of about $5.5 million, has two distinct nines. The front nine is mostly open, tracking through prairie land. The back nine is cut out of a lovely hardwood forest on the cusp of the non-glaciated Driftless Area to the west.

Had things moved more quickly, the course would have been at a different location and perhaps been designed by George Fazio or the team of Ken Killian and Dick Nugent. After all, the UW had been discussing such a thing since the early 1950s. The latest, successful version of the project was revived in 1983, following a gift from the will of Carl

UNIVERSITY RIDGE

5,005 to 6,888* yards
par 72
rating 73.2
slope 142

ARCHITECT
Robert Trent Jones Jr.

CALL
(608) 845-7700

WEB SITE
www.universityridge.com

ADDRESS
9002 County Road PD,
Verona, WI 53593

DIRECTIONS
Located south of Madison's Beltline Highway 12-18, take Highway 18/151 south two miles, then travel west on County Road PD for three miles. Club is on north side of PD.

*Yardage extension planned.

Dietze of Madison, who wished his money to be used for a university golf course. In 1986, another committee was formed, and Jones got the job.

Course lengthening, to better accommodate top tournaments, and a nine-hole practice course, were approved by the University Board of Regents in 2005. About a year after that, school officials said plans for the "academy course" to be built next to the original 18 had been delayed, but that lengthening the Jones design and enhancing existing practice facilities were still planned. The course is home to the University of Wisconsin golf teams and the state high school championships.

The course, as is, pleases most customers because of its beauty and playability. The course is difficult, but not penal. There's almost always a bailout spot to hit to. But if you gamble, and hit a bad shot, you'll certainly lose strokes—and likely a few golf balls in the process.

A great example of a risk-reward hole is number two, a 546-yard par 5 that can be reached in two by long hitters blasting from an elevated tee. But to get into position for an eagle, you have to drive over a rock-strewn gully and big traps to a slender landing area with trees on the right. And then you have to hit to a slender green surrounded by deep rough, woods, sand and some towering trees.

Another great risk-reward opportunity is the signature hole, number 16, which features 16 sand hazards. The 533-yard holes go down, then up and to the right around bunkers and an uncut meadow. It features two routes to a narrow, windswept green. You can take the shortcut over the trees and to a lower fairway for a shorter but intimidating shot over a field of bunkers. Or you can take the longer route up the left-hand side, avoiding trees but in the vicinity of some big bunkers and mounds, setting yourself up for a short iron into the green. Either way, the uphill approach is often obscured, making the flagstick hard to see.

There's little reward for trying to cut the corner at another memorable hole, the par 4, 413 18th, one of the state's best finishing holes. This dogleg left plays a lot longer than advertised, and those trying to cut the corner likely will end up in deep rough or a tough lie in the sand. Hit to the corner and try to bounce a long iron or fairway wood onto the 120-foot deep green at the top of the hill. Patience is rewarded on this hole, just as patience was rewarded for all those years of waiting for a UW golf course.

HOLE TO BEAT
Number four, par 4, 444 yards

The numbers all say 4 on this hole, but you'll need some luck to write that number down. The tee shot is uphill and over a ridge on the windswept front nine to a tiny landing area that tilts right, toward Morse Pond. A row of trees guards the left rough. The approach shot is severely uphill and often blind. Again, don't go right, where sand traps and trees wait to gobble up errant iron shots. The green has two tiers, but it's plenty deep to hold a long second shot.

Washington
County Golf Course

HARTFORD

Think of hills when you play Washington County Golf Course—for the terrain, for the architect and for a famous nearby landmark.

The citizens of southeast Wisconsin's Washington County can brag about the WCGC's nationally known designer (Arthur Hills), a top-notch practice facility (kids play for free on the three-hole practice course when with an adult), the amenities of a semiprivate club (locker rooms) and views to rival just about any golf course in the state (keep reading).

Yes, Washington County Golf Course is a municipal golf course, but you'd never know it.

The first tee and the well-appointed clubhouse sit high atop a hill north of Hartford, located northwest of Milwaukee in the glacially formed Kettle Moraines. From the clubhouse snack bar, you can feast upon the panorama that includes another hilltop landmark—the National Shrine of Mary at Holy Hill. Grab

WASHINGTON COUNTY GOLF COURSE

5,200 to 7,007 yards
par 72
rating 73.1
slope 130

ARCHITECT
Arthur Hills

CALL
(888) 383-4653

WEB SITE
www.golfwcgc.com

ADDRESS
6439 Clover Road,
Hartford, WI 53027

DIRECTIONS
From U.S. Highway 41, take Route 60 west to Hartford, turn north on Route 83 and travel one mile to Clover Road.

some inspiration from this more than century-old religious complex rising 1,350 feet above sea level as you tackle Hills' fine design.

Hills molded 175 acres of wetland and former farmland into a championship course with municipal rates. The course, built for about $7 million, opened in 1997 and now plays host to a variety of regional tournaments.

Despite a virtually treeless landscape, Hills designed a memorable course that will test every facet of your game. Let's hope they never plant a lot of trees on this course; there's plenty of trouble already.

Among the hazards: more than 50 sand traps, four big water hazards, many mounds topped with high grass, three walls made of boulders gathered during the construction process, and the wind, which always seems to be a factor.

Here's hoping your tee shots are always downwind at Washington County Golf Course. Because if they aren't, some of the long par 4s can be brutal. And Hills fashioned quite a few long par 4s. Number one is 417 yards from the back tees, number two is 449 yards, number nine is 450 yards, number 12 is 455 yards, number 15 is 411 yards and number 18 is 405 yards. And just for good measure, numbers nine and 18 are steep uphill doglegs with plenty of sand.

The par 3s are tough, too, especially the 197-yard 14th hole, which has a pond flanking the left part of the green and the 222-yard par 3 16th. Hills also placed big ponds on numbers seven and eight. Number eight is a 334-yard par 4 that doglegs left around water in the lower part of the course; take a chance over the water and you'll significantly shorten the approach shot.

Long par 5s also are course hallmarks. Two par 5s on the back—numbers 13 and 17—both measure more than 550 yards. But almost everybody agrees that the toughest par 5 and toughest hole is the sweeping dogleg number seven measuring 545 yards.

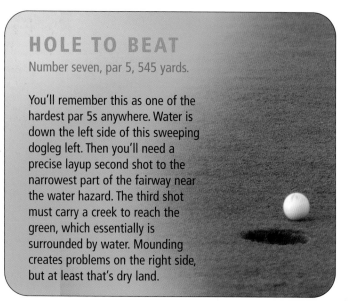

HOLE TO BEAT

Number seven, par 5, 545 yards.

You'll remember this as one of the hardest par 5s anywhere. Water is down the left side of this sweeping dogleg left. Then you'll need a precise layup second shot to the narrowest part of the fairway near the water hazard. The third shot must carry a creek to reach the green, which essentially is surrounded by water. Mounding creates problems on the right side, but at least that's dry land.

The Straits at
Whistling Straits

HAVEN

How do you pick the best course out of a quartet crafted by Pete Dye and Kohler Co. chair Herbert V. Kohler? The nod has to go to Whistling Straits, because that seaside links layout is the one that hosted the PGA Championship in 2004 (winner Vijay Singh), will host the 2007 U.S. Senior Open and is on tap to stage the 2010 and 2015 PGA Championships and the 43rd Ryder Cup Matches in 2020.

So while the two Blackwolf Run courses in the well-kept burg of Kohler along the mighty Sheboygan River (Meadow Valleys and the River, site of the 1998 U.S. Women's Open) and the Irish course up the coast (companion to the Straits course) are well worth playing, everybody wants to play the course that Dye and Kohler built along the Lake Michigan shoreline atop a transformed piece of old military land. And who can blame them for wanting to

THE STRAITS AT WHISTLING STRAITS

5,396 to 7,362 yards
par 72
rating 76.7
slope 151

ARCHITECT
Pete Dye

CALL
(800) 618-5535

WEB SITE
www.destinationkohler.com

ADDRESS
N8501 County LS,
Sheboygan, WI 53083

DIRECTIONS
From Interstate 43 north- or southbound, exit 128 east. Travel east and take the first left—North 40th Street becomes Dairyland Drive—continue four miles north to County FF. Turn right (east) onto County FF, proceed one mile to Whistling Straits entrance.

walk (which you must) with a caddy in the footsteps of the best modern male players?

So the Straits course, which opened in July 1998, is the first among equals in Kohler's magic Wisconsin golf kingdom—an international venue to go along with Kohler's more recent purchase and refurbishment of the Old Course Hotel and the Duke's golf course in St. Andrews, Scotland.

In Kohler, many golfing visitors stay at the luxurious American Club resort—which some have dubbed the Pinehurst of the North.

It all comes together in a delightful package that has earned the Straits a ranking of number 23 among America's 100 Greatest Golf Courses by *Golf Digest.*

Kohler's got the details down to a tee—from its own well-appointed bathroom fixtures to the Irish-styled stone clubhouse to the caddies and Scottish black-faced sheep that roam a treeless scene noted for its high grasses, fescue fairways, dunes, big untended sandy areas and pot bunkers.

The ambiance rates a birdie. The golf—a hole in one. About the only thing missing is salt air. The golf course and the many lake views are unparalleled in the Midwest. The eight holes along Lake Michigan, including four memorable par 3s, are superb.

Many matches will be decided at the two finishing holes. First comes the 223-yard 17th, where even a good tee shot can land in the lake and ruin a good score. The left side of the green and fairway drop abruptly into sand, rocks and water. The right side is blocked by a sloping piece of rough punctuated by a couple of pot bunkers. Mix in a little wind and a wager, and even those with steady nerves will be twitching a bit.

That's followed by a monster of a par 4. The 489-yard

18th heads away from the lake to the clubhouse over a 200-yard carry into a prevailing wind uphill over a grass-topped dunescape and then over a creek to an elevated green set into a bunkered embankment.

Pricey. Frustrating. But worth the adventure. Tip your caddy, compose yourself, grab a Guinness in the clubhouse and congratulate yourself on a seaside golf trip to an international venue in Wisconsin. Think of the airfare you saved.

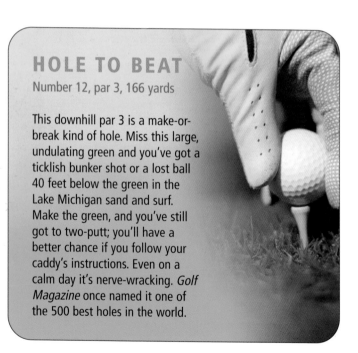

HOLE TO BEAT
Number 12, par 3, 166 yards

This downhill par 3 is a make-or-break kind of hole. Miss this large, undulating green and you've got a ticklish bunker shot or a lost ball 40 feet below the green in the Lake Michigan sand and surf. Make the green, and you've still got to two-putt; you'll have a better chance if you follow your caddy's instructions. Even on a calm day it's nerve-wracking. *Golf Magazine* once named it one of the 500 best holes in the world.

Wild Ridge
Golf Course
EAU CLAIRE

In Eau Claire, downtown actually is down—at the city's lowest elevation near the confluence of the Chippewa and Eau Claire rivers. Travel perpendicular to the river, and you go up, out of the Chippewa Valley, as the region is known. Head west about five miles, and you'll find a windswept plain the locals call Truax Prairie, named for one of the early settlers.

You'll also find a nearly treeless, windswept golf course. In the late 1990s, the owners of the 18-hole Mill Run public course wanted something a little more special than their tidy 6,000-yard layout. They didn't have to go far. Behind their clubhouse was a wooded ridge that fell away to farmland. So they hired Illinois architect Greg Martin and in 1999 opened something special, a 7,034-yard gem called Wild Ridge.

Wild Ridge isn't one of Wisconsin's best-known destination courses, but it can stack up with the best of them in terms of beauty, playability and difficulty. "Wild Ridge engages golfers in three ways—visual, strategic and

WILD RIDGE GOLF COURSE

5,280 to 7,034 yards
par 72
rating 73.6
slope 130

ARCHITECT
Greg Martin

CALL
(715) 834-1766

WEB SITE
www.wildridgegolf.com

ADDRESS
3905 Kane Road, Eau Claire, WI 54703

DIRECTIONS
From Interstate 94, take exit 59, go east to County TT (Kane Road) and turn right to the entrance.

recreational. I assimilate the golf course into the landscape. I use the surrounding terrain and let the golf hole feed off it," said Martin, who also designed the acclaimed Rich Harvest private course in Chicago. "(Wild Ridge) feels good. It looks good. It plays well."

The focal point of the course is a ridge top, where a modest clubhouse affords panoramic views of the prairie. With bookend par 4 first and 10th tees atop the ridge, Wild Ridge drops into an open valley, where a variety of fun begins.

Wild Ridge seems to demand something different on each hole. The front nine has a beast in a 657-yard par 5 called Sherman's March (next to Sherman Creek) but also a breather in a 150-yard, downhill par 3 cut from a hillside. It has seven holes that play around water or marshy areas and at least two tiers on every green.

It's the easier of the two nines. The hilly back is more susceptible to the wind and can take the sails out of your score. The only flat hole on the back, the 211-yard 17th, is at the top of the ridge and can be impossible if the prevailing wind is up. But the view is worth the trek.

The back has a nice mix of birdie holes on three short but tricky par 4s and a few holes that could ruin your round. The latter include the 533-yard par 5 14th traversing an upland with trouble left and right, the lengthy 480-yard, par 4 15th and 439-yard par 4 18th, a ridge-to-valley special that sums up the wild ride at Wild Ridge.

Aesthetically pleasing, Wild Ridge has 60 sand traps, 60 acres of wetland areas and a waterfall. "I love the dramatic elevation changes, the contoured greens and the great diversity of holes, scenery and challenges," said David Longville, director of operations at Wild Ridge.

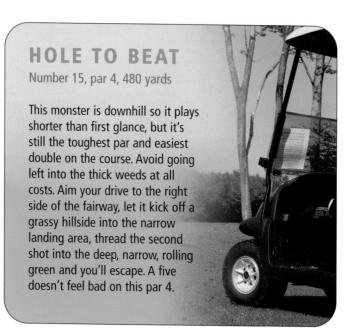

HOLE TO BEAT
Number 15, par 4, 480 yards

This monster is downhill so it plays shorter than first glance, but it's still the toughest par and easiest double on the course. Avoid going left into the thick weeds at all costs. Aim your drive to the right side of the fairway, let it kick off a grassy hillside into the narrow landing area, thread the second shot into the deep, narrow, rolling green and you'll escape. A five doesn't feel bad on this par 4.

Wild Rock Golf Club

WISCONSIN DELLS

Golfers who show up at Wilderness Resort and hardly recognize the place can be excused. In the 1990s, the 6,629-yard Wilderness Woods golf course replaced the 1920s-era Dell View course as part of an $8.5 million resort expansion.

And in mid- to late summer 2007, the new Wild Rock Golf Club is scheduled to open, replacing Wilderness Woods as part of yet another multimillion-dollar expansion at the popular hotel-condo-waterpark resort.

But don't expect Wild Rock to be replaced anytime soon. This course, designed by noted architects Michael Hurdzan and Dana Fry, likely will rank among the best places to play in Wisconsin and will more than do its part to bring more tourists to Wisconsin Dells.

WILD ROCK GOLF CLUB

5,156 to 7,411 yards
par 72
rating 76.3
slope 140

ARCHITECTS
Michael Hurdzan and Dana Fry

CALL
(608) 253-4653

WEB SITE
www.wildrockgolf.com

ADDRESS
511 E. Adams St., Wisconsin Dells, WI 53965

DIRECTIONS
From Interstate 90-94, take exit 92. Travel east on Route 12 one mile to the resort entrance and follow the signs.

Construction at Wild Rock began in September of 2005 after the owners of Wilderness bought 200 acres of adjacent, rolling land and set their sights on creating a first-class championship course. Based on the facts—par 72, 7,411 yards and a slope of 140—they succeeded.

The proof, of course, is how it plays. Hurdzan and Fry, who also designed the acclaimed Troy Burne and Erin Hills in Wisconsin, had several major geographic features at their disposal. They included a boulder-strewn stream and accompanying ravine, a dry streambed, thick stands of hardwoods, a ridgeline that offers great views and significant elevation changes—plus an unexpected bonus, an old quarry.

"It uses the topography of the Wisconsin Dells area pretty uniquely. This is truly a championship golf course," said Chris Goodwick, PGA pro and general manager of resort golf operations. "It will blow the old course away."

Nine holes of Wilderness Woods, mostly the front nine, have been preserved as The Woods, designed for families and the less serious golfer, Goodwick said, giving the resort 27 total golf holes.

With varied topography and great views, Wild Rock will have something for everyone. Several early holes are wooded, with two of them crossing ravines, including the 464-yard par 4 third hole. The course then climbs a high ridge, reaching it at the number five green. You get the full view from the next tee; at the start of the brawny 588-yard, par 5 sixth hole, you can see for 25 miles toward the grand Wisconsin River valley. The sixth, the longest par 5 on the course, has woods lurking off the right side and ticks to the right at the end to a slightly elevated green protected by a pot bunker.

Much of the back nine, holes 12 through 16, play in, around and through the old rock quarry, which was left mostly as it was found. An unlucky hook or pull will disappear into the quarry on the 13th, a par 4 measuring 453 yards. The 15th, 179 yards, has nothing but quarry, 50 to 60 feet below, between the tee and green.

Water, including a man-made lake and the stream, is on four holes. Add that feature to the mixed terrain at Wild Rock and it adds up to a course that will withstand the test of time, unlike its predecessors.

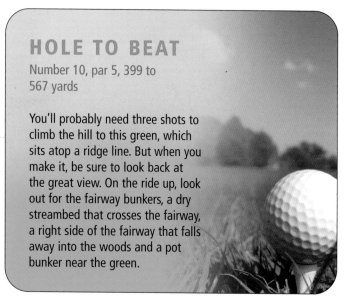

HOLE TO BEAT
Number 10, par 5, 399 to 567 yards

You'll probably need three shots to climb the hill to this green, which sits atop a ridge line. But when you make it, be sure to look back at the great view. On the ride up, look out for the fairway bunkers, a dry streambed that crosses the fairway, a right side of the fairway that falls away into the woods and a pot bunker near the green.

Fifty (and One) More
Fun Places to Play

Playing golf in Wisconsin is challenging, fun and usually very affordable. While you've just read about our picks for the 25 top courses around the state, here's a sampling of 50 other fun places to play the grand old game. Wisconsin public courses owe their unique feel to Mother Nature and architects including Pete Dye, Robert Trent Jones Sr., Robert Trent Jones Jr., Tom Bendelow, Lawrence and Roger Packard, Art Johnson, Joel Goldstrand, Rick Jacobson, Bob Lohmann, Jerry Matthews, Robert Bruce Harris, Bob Cupp, David and Garrett Gill, Ken Killian and Dick Nugent as well as playing greats like Arnold Palmer, Gary Player, Jack Nicklaus, Lee Trevino and Andy North.

For more on golfing in Wisconsin, try these Web links: www.travelwisconsin.com/golf/dream.htm, www.wisgolfer.com, www.wsga.org and www.wisconsin4golf.com.

From the Lake Superior shore to the Illinois border, golf in Wisconsin never has been better. Come with us on our most excellent golf adventure.

1. At **Apostle Highlands** in **Bayfield**, your first shot must carry Lake Superior. Well, not the big lake, but a large pond shaped like the lake and built to scale—and including a lighthouse! No mulligans if you don't reach Canada. You can see far and wide over the real Lake Superior from the course 500 feet above it all.

   (877) 222-4053, (715) 779-5960
   www.golfbayfield.com

2. At **Forest Point Resort and Golf Course in Gordon**, dating to 1932, the old sand greens have been transformed. On this nine-hole course, you will play one of the largest greens, 12,000 square feet, and one of the smallest, 1,000 square feet, in the state. On the fifth hole, watch out for the "meteor pond." If it sucks up your ball, blame the heavens.

   (715) 376-2322 www.forestpoint.com

3. At **Trout Lake Golf and Country Club** in **Arbor Vitae** near Minocqua, you have a chance to drive the green—and hit the old farmhouse turned clubhouse—on the 260-yard par 4 number 18 finishing hole. Relax after the round on the classic porch. It's a Northwoods favorite.

   (715) 385-2189 www.troutlakegolf.com

4. At **Plum Lake Golf Course** in **Sayner** golfers can't see the green on the 150-yard fourth hole, but a 15-foot flagstick helps for directions to what the locals call the "sugar bowl" green. Swap stories later in the log lodge clubhouse.

   (715) 542-2598 www.plumlakegolfclub.com

5.   At **Lake Forest Golf Course** in **Eagle River,** you can tee it up on the same short resort course that has entertained vacationers such as Dwight Eisenhower, Elizabeth Taylor and Joan Crawford.

(800) 830-0471, (715) 479-3251
www.lakeforestvacations.com

6.   At wild **Teal Wing Golf Club** near **Hayward**, you might hear the bugling of elk or the splash of a big musky hitting a surface lure while playing through dense forests and bogs that characterize the land around the rustic Ross' Teal Lake Lodge. Concentrate on the scenery, not the lost balls you'll incur on this difficult course.

(715) 462-9051 www.teallake.com

7. At **Voyager Village Country Club** near **Danbury,** 17 holes wind through the Northwoods. The exception is the 505-yard 6th hole. It runs along a cement airstrip, which is out of bounds, costing you stroke, distance and all your frequent flyer miles.

    (800) 782-0329, (715) 259-3910
    www.voyagervillage.com

8. At **Spooner Golf Club** in **Spooner,** the signature finishing hole is a 396-yard par 4 beauty featuring a fairway doglegging and sloping along a wetland all the way to the green. The 18th, part of the original nine, was designed in the 1930s by Thomas Vardon of White Bear Lake, Minnesota, brother of British golf legend Harry Vardon.

    (888) 635-3580, (715) 635-3580
    www.spoonergolf.com

9. At **Gateway Golf Course** in far north **Land O' Lakes,** you literally can hit a ball into another state. The third tee is in Wisconsin, and the fairway is in the Upper Peninsula of Michigan.

    (715) 547-3929

10. At **Tagalong Golf Resort** in **Birchwood,** you're stepping in the footsteps of millionaire businessman Frank Stout, who opened his St. Andrews-inspired course in August 1925 with a match between the reigning U.S. Open and British Open champs. The old links layout along Red Cedar Lake has since been augmented with a new nine holes. Guests at Stout's

nearby island lodge access this classic resort by boat.

(800) 657-4843, (715) 354-3458

www.tagalonggolf.com

11. At **Forest Hills Golf Course** in **La Crosse**, one of the oldest in Wisconsin dating to 1901, you play beneath the Mississippi River city's most famous landmark—Granddad Bluff.

(608) 779-4653 www.foresthillslacrosse.com

12. At **St. Croix National** in **Somerset**, if you have the feeling this land could be used for skiing in the winter, you'd be right: It once was Snowcrest downhill ski area. Now your ball runs down old ski runs, thanks to designer Joel Goldstrand.

(715) 247-4200 www.wpgolf.com/stcroix

13 & 14. At **Baraboo Country Club** in **Baraboo** and **Koshkonong Mounds** near **Fort Atkinson**, you often play around ancient effigy mounds built by some of the original inhabitants of Wisconsin.

Baraboo Country Club (800) 657-4981, (608) 3568195 www.baraboocountryclub.com

Koshkonong Mounds (920) 563-2823 www.koshkonongmounds.com

15. At **Devil's Head Resort** in **Merrimac** the golf course next to the ski resort features spectacular views and an old three-foot-high stone wall that runs through the

13th and 14th holes. Signs warn: "Beware of ricochet."

(800) 472-6670 www.devilsheadresort.com

16. **Tuscumbia Country Club** in **Green Lake**, founded in 1896, bills itself as the oldest course in the state. There is some controversy here, as venerable Janesville Country Club traces its roots to 1894. No matter, walk down history past tall pines, oaks and maples and view Native American memorabilia in the dark-paneled clubhouse.

(920) 294-3381 www.tuscumbiacc.com

17. At **Scharenberg's White Lake Golf Resort** near **Montello**, you may not make a birdie but you may get lucky enough to see one. Peacocks often can be seen wandering the course.

(608) 297-2255 www.wisvacations.com/scharenbergs

18. **At Quit Qui Oc Golf Club** in **Elkhart Lake**, experience a fun round on this tight course with rolling fairways and small greens before or after taking in the races at Road America. The course dates back to 1927 on a design by Tom Bendelow, a prolific course architect.

(920) 876-2833 www.quitquioc.com

19. **Shorewood Golf Course** in **Green Bay,** on a pretty tract of land near Lake Michigan, gave up nine of its holes years ago for the building of the University of Wisconsin–Green Bay. But it'll require several trips before you go to school on the nine tricky, shaded

greens remaining.

(920) 465-2118 www.uwgb.edu/shorewood

20. **The Bergamont Golf Club** in **Oregon** south of Madison is the first solo 18-hole design of two-time U.S. Open champion Andy North of Madison, who also was part of the North Nine at the House on the Rock Resort and Trappers Turn in Wisconsin Dells. The 17th hole, which plays up to 197 yards, is a testy downhill par 3 with water all along the left side. *Golf Digest*, in its January 2007 issue, put Bergamont number seven on its list of best new public courses under $75. But an ownership dispute in late 2006 cast doubts on the future of the high-end development and course.

(608) 835-6900 www.thebergamont.com

21. **Whispering Springs** in **Fond du Lac**, opened in 1997, is a splendid layout perched atop the western edge of the Niagara Escarpment, a geologic feature that forms Door County and runs all the way to the big falls on the New York-Ontario border.

(920) 921-8053 www.whisperingspringsgolf.com

22. At the **Squires Country Club** in **Port Washington**, try your luck on the 250-yard, par 3 17th near Lake Michigan. It's one of the longest par 3s in the state.

(262) 285-3402 www.squirescc.com

23 & 24. **Missing Links** in **Mequon** is one of the state's best executive courses, opened in 1984 for use with the

Cayman golf ball (a short-lived ball designed to fly half the distances of the normal golf ball).

(262) 243-5711 www.missinglinksmequon.com

Another good executive course is **Spring Creek** in **Whitewater.**

(920) 563-4499 www.springcreekgolf.com

25. **Old Hickory** in **Beaver Dam**, one of our favorites, started from a Tom Bendelow design that later was enhanced by a plan done in part by Bill Sixty Jr., son of the old *Milwaukee Journal* golf columnist. Bobby Brue, a Wisconsin trick-shot artist who played on the Senior Tour, shot a two-under par 70 to open the refurbished course in 1968.

(920) 887-7577 www.oldhickorycc.com

26. **Rainbow Springs, Mukwonago**, never succeeded as a resort, but its course is still known as one of the toughest around. Site of the Women's Western Open won by LPGA great Mickey Wright in 1966, the course has no sand traps but copious amounts of water. (262) 363-4550

27. At **George Williams Golf Course, Williams Bay**, part of the course runs through University of Chicago property occupied by the Yerkes Observatory, the world's largest refracting telescope. Dr. James Naismith, inventor of basketball, laid out the course. (262) 245-9507

28. **Kettle Moraine,** near **Dousman** on the edge of the southern Kettle Moraine State Forest, was built a few holes at a time by the original owner, Dewey Laak. He and Mother Nature fashioned a scenic and fun course. (262) 965-6200 www.kettlemorainegolf.com

29. **Eagle Springs Golf Resort, Eagle**, is a nine-hole course you'll never forget. An apple tree grows through the roof of the clubhouse, and you hit from glacial mound to glacial mound on the 134-yard par 3 second "volcano hole." The course's first two holes are credited to Chicago's A.G. Spaulding, founder of the sporting goods company. (262) 594-2462 www.eaglespringsgolfresort.com

30. Pete Dye and Jack Nicklaus combined to design the

old Briar Patch Course in **Lake Geneva** in 1971. Since then, the old Playboy resort has been transformed by Marcus Corp. and the course has been redesigned by Bob Cupp and renamed **The Highlands.**

(800) 558-3417 wwwgrandgeneva.com

31.   The land for the Kenosha Co. municipal complex at **Brighton Dale Links** came via the federal government, which once contemplated building a Cold War-era military air base north of Chicago. Now 36 holes are near the 4,500-acre Bong Recreation Area.

(262) 878-1440
www.co.Kenosha.wi.us/publicworks/golf

32.   **Shoop Park Golf Course,** a nine-holer in **Racine,** is right on Lake Michigan next to the Wind Point Lighthouse.

(262) 681-9714 www.racinegolfonline.com

33. **Riverside Golf Club** in **Janesville** is a muni gem that plays primarily to a 1946 redesign by Robert Bruce Harris. Some of the best holes are on a bluff over the Rock River and others wind through troublesome, low-slung but pretty flowering crabapple trees.

    (608) 757-3088 www.janesville-golf.com

34. You'll often see sandhill cranes and other special bird life at the linksy **Meadows of Six Mile Creek** that winds through marshland in **Waunakee**.

    (608) 849-9000
    www.madisongolf.com/meadows.php

35. At **Glenway Golf Course**, a nine-hole muni course in **Madison**, two holes feature stoplights. You don't hit your drive until you get the green light.

    (608) 266-4736

36, 37 & 38. Famous PGA pros have made their marks in Wisconsin. Tiger Woods had his first pro hole-in-one in 1996 during the PGA Tour stop at **Brown Deer Park** (browndeergolfclub.com), using a six-iron to traverse 202 yards. Jack Nicklaus shot 70 at **Odana Hills Golf Club** in Madison in an exhibition round (608) 266-4724, www.ci.madison.wi.us/parks/golf/odana/odana.

Steve Stricker grew up playing **Towne Country Club** in **Edgerton** (608) 884-4231.

39. **Shawano Lake Golf Club,** first opened in 1922, used to be called Shalagoco. That's not an Indian word but a combination of letters from the current name. Look for the osprey nesting platform near the number eight green.

(715) 524-4890 www.shalagoco.com

40 & 41. At the **Irish Course** north of **Kohler** www.destinationkohler.com; (800) 618-5535, Pete Dye designed a blind par 3 hole. **Erin Hills** northwest of **Milwaukee** has one, too www.erinhills.com; (866) 724-8822.

42. At **Timber Terrace Golf Course** in **Chippewa Falls** the third hole has a sawdust trap, the remnants of an old sawmill along the Chippewa River.

(715) 726-1500.

43, 44 & 45. At **Lake Wisconsin Country Club** in **Prairie du Sac**, at **Portage Country Club** in **Portage** and at **Lakeshore Golf Course** in **Oshkosh**, you sometimes feel like you have one foot in the water. All three feature memorable holes on lakes. Lakeshore's number nine, 220-yard par 3 starts on a tee jutting into Lake Butte des Morts; the back tees on Lake Wisconsin's 169-yard par 3 12th could be on its island tee box; and Portage's 242-yard par 3 third hole is along Swan Lake.

Lake Wisconsin (608) 643-2405
www.lakewisconsincc.com

Portage (608) 742-5121 www.portagecc.net

Lakeshore (920) 235-6200

46 & 47. At least two Wisconsin courses make the most of nine holes. At **New Richmond Links** in **New Richmond**, you can play the course forward or backward. At **Thornberry Creek Country Club** in **Oneida**, the original nine holes, built in an old sand pit as part of a Rick Jacobson design, features double greens (like Madeline Island Golf Club) so you can play it twice without getting bored.

New Richmond (715) 246-6724
www.nrgolfclub.com

Thornberry Creek (920) 434-7501
www.thornberrycreekcc.net

48 & 49 At the **Alpine Resort Golf Course** in **Door County's Egg Harbor,** golfers for years took a tram to see the

view of Lake Michigan's Green Bay from the tee of the 268-yard dramatically downhill, par 4 ninth hole. No more, but the spectacular view remains. And after the ninth hole at **Hallie Golf Club** near **Eau Claire,** visitors have long enjoyed a cable car ride and the view of Lake Hallie and the mighty Chippewa River.

Alpine (920) 868-3000 www.alpineresort.com

Hallie (715) 723-8524

50 & 51 At **Lake Breeze Golf Course** in **Winneconne** and **Christmas Mountain** in **the Dells,** you will play greens shaped like the state of Wisconsin. Golf, Wisconsin—the two words just go together.

Lake Breeze (920) 582-7585

Christmas Mountain (608) 254-3971
www.christmasmountainvillage.com

Jeff Mayers is president of WisPolitics Publishing in Madison, Wisconsin, and co-author of two previous golf guide books and *Exploring Wisconsin Trout Streams.* He also was a contributor to Tom Wendelburg's *Catching Big Fish on Light Fly Tackle.*

Jerry Poling is the news-wire editor and a columnist for the *Eau Claire Leader Telegram* and co-author of *Wisconsin Golf Getaways.* He also is the author of *After They Were Packers: The Super Bowl XXXI Champs & Other Green Bay Legends, Downfield!: Untold Stories of the Green Bay Packers,* and *Summer Up North: Henry Aaron and the Legend of Eau Claire Baseball.*